W9-AHM-851

Math Expressions

Volume 1

**Developed by
The Children's Math Worlds
Research Project**

PROJECT DIRECTOR AND AUTHOR

Dr. Karen C. Fuson

This material is based upon work supported by the
National Science Foundation
under Grant Numbers
ESI-9816320, REC-9806020, and RED-935373.

Any opinions, findings, and conclusions or recommendations expressed in this
material are those of the author and do not necessarily reflect the views of the
National Science Foundation.

HOUGHTON MIFFLIN   BOSTON

Teacher Reviewers

Kindergarten
Patricia Stroh Sugiyama
Wilmette, Illinois

Barbara Wahle
Evanston, Illinois

Grade 1
Sandra Budson
Newton, Massachusetts

Janet Pecci
Chicago, Illinois

Megan Rees
Chicago, Illinois

Grade 2
Molly Dunn
Danvers, Massachusetts

Agnes Lesnick
Hillside, Illinois

Rita Soto
Chicago, Illinois

Grade 3
Jane Curran
Honesdale, Pennsylvania

Sandra Tucker
Chicago, Illinois

Grade 4
Sara Stoneberg Llibre
Chicago, Illinois

Sheri Roedel
Chicago, Illinois

Grade 5
Todd Atler
Chicago, Illinois

Leah Barry
Norfolk, Massachusetts

Special Thanks

Special thanks to the many teachers, students, parents, principals, writers, researchers, and work-study students who participated in the Children's Math Worlds Research Project over the years.

Credits

Cover art: (arctic fox) © Mike Macri/Masterfile. (bridge) © Photodisc/Getty Images
Illustrative art: Dave Klug
Technical art: Morgan-Cain & Associates

Printed in the U.S.A.

ISBN-13: 978-0-618-50988-1
ISBN-10: 0-618-50988-7

8 9 1421 11 10 09

VOLUME 1 CONTENTS

Mini Unit B Lines, Angles, and Triangles

Unit 3 Multi-Digit Multiplication

Multiplication With Tens

Multiplication by One-Digit Numbers

Multiplication by Two-Digit Numbers

Multiplication With Hundreds and Thousands

*This lesson consists only of activities from the Teacher's Guide.

Mini Unit C The Metric Measurement System

Class Activity

Name _____

Date _____

► Use the Target

X	1	2	3	4	5	6	7	8	9	10
1	1	2	3	4	5	6	7	8	9	10
2	2	4	6	8	10	12	14	16	18	20
3	3	6	9	12	15	18	21	24	27	30
4	4	8	12	16	20	24	28	32	36	40
5	5	10	15	20	25	30	35	40	45	50
6	6	12	18	24	30	36	42	48	54	60
7	7	14	21	28	35	42	49	56	63	70
8	8	16	24	32	40	48	56	64	72	80
9	9	18	27	36	45	54	63	72	81	90
10	10	20	30	40	50	60	70	80	90	100

1. Discuss how you can use the Target to find the product for 5 × 8.

2. Discuss how you can use the Target to practice division.

3. Practice using the Target.

4. **On the Back** When using the Target, how are multiplication and division alike? How are they different?

Dear Family,

Your child is learning math in an innovative program called *Math Expressions*. Your child will learn math and have fun by:

- working with different objects and making drawings of various math situations.
- working with other students and sharing problem-solving strategies with them.
- writing and solving problems and connecting math to their daily lives.

At the beginning of this unit, your child will be learning the basics of multiplication and division. One learning tool is the "count-by." Using fingers can help.

2s count-bys

2 4 6 8 10 12

- Multiplication is a fast way to count same-size groups: $2 + 2 + 2 + 2 + 2 + 2 = 12$ is the same as 6 groups of 2, so we can say $6 \times 2 = 12$. To find 6×2, we "count-by" 2 and raise 1 finger 6 times: 2, 4, 6, 8, 10, 12. The last number we say is 12, so we know that $6 \times 2 = 12$.

- Division is the reverse of multiplication: $6 \times 2 = 12$ written as division is $12 \div 2 = 6$ or $12 \div 6 = 2$. To find $12 \div 2$, we "count-by" 2 up to 12 and keep track of how many fingers we raise. We raise 6 fingers to get to 12, so we know that $12 \div 2 = 6$.

It is vital that your child learn the basic multiplications and divisions. He or she must have a regular time and quiet place for practice every night.

Sincerely,
Your child's teacher

Estimada familia:

Su niño está aprendiendo matemáticas con un programa innovador llamado *Math Expressions*. Su niño aprenderá matemáticas y se divertirá mientras:

- trabaja con varios objetos y hace dibujos de problemas matemáticos.
- trabaja con otros estudiantes y comparte estrategias para resolver problemas.
- escribe y resuelve problemas, y los relaciona con su vida diaria.

Al principio de esta unidad su niño aprenderá las reglas básicas de la multiplicación y de la división. Una buena herramienta de aprendizaje es "contar de cierto número en cierto número." Su niño puede usar los dedos para ayudarse.

contar de 2 en 2

| 2 | 4 | 6 | 8 | 10 | 12 |

- La multiplicación es una manera rápida de contar grupos del mismo tamaño: $2 + 2 + 2 + 2 + 2 + 2 = 12$ es lo mismo que 6 grupos de 2, entonces podemos decir $6 \times 2 = 12$. Para hallar 6×2 contamos de 2 en 2 y levantamos un dedo 6 veces: 2, 4, 6, 8, 10, 12. El último número que decimos es 12, por lo tanto sabemos que $6 \times 2 = 12$.

- La división es lo contrario de la multiplicación: $6 \times 2 = 12$, escrito como división es $12 \div 2 = 6$ ó $12 \div 6 = 2$. Para hallar $12 \div 2$, contamos de 2 en 2 hasta el 12 y observamos cuántos dedos levantamos. Para llegar a 12 levantamos 6 dedos, por lo tanto sabemos que $12 \div 2 = 6$.

Es importante que su niño aprenda las multiplicaciones y divisiones básicas. Debe tener un horario y un lugar tranquilo para practicar todas las noches.

Atentamente,
El maestro de su niño

Patterns in 2s, 5s, 10s, and 9s

► Look at a Product in Four Ways

David picked some apples. He could have counted them one by one, but he thought he could use multiplication to count them faster.

He arranged the apples in four different ways, and found the same total each time.

Write a multiplication equation to represent each picture.

1.

_____

2.

_____

3.

_____

4.

_____

5. You have learned that multiplication is a way of finding the total in equal groups. Can you see or make equal groups in all four pictures? Explain.

_____

_____

_____

Class Activity

▶ Introduce Arrays

An **array** is an arrangement of objects in rows and columns. Each row has the same number of items, and each column has the same number of items. This array has 2 rows and 6 columns. We say it is a 2-by-6 array.

6 columns
2 rows • • • • • • 2 by 6 array

6. Write a multiplication equation for this array. _____

Make a drawing to show each array and then write a multiplication equation to represent the total number of objects.

7. 3 by 5

8. 8 by 2

9. 3 by 9

_____   _____   _____

10. 4 by 5

11. 2 by 10

12. 5 by 10

_____   _____   _____

13. **Math Journal** The total number of objects is 18. Make two different arrays showing this total. Then write a multiplication equation for each array.

Class Activity

▶ **Commutativity with Arrays and Groups**

Vocabulary
Commutative Property of Multiplication

The **Commutative Property of Multiplication** states that changing the order of the factors in a multiplication problem does not change the product. So, for any numbers a and b, the Commutative Property states that $a \times b = b \times a$.

14. How do these arrays show the Commutative Property for 2×3?

_____

_____

15. Explain how you could use arrays to show the Commutative Property for any two whole number factors.

_____

_____

_____

_____

16. On page 5, David arranged his groups of apples to form arrays. Do you think you could always arrange same-size groups to form arrays? Why or why not?

_____

_____

17. Is the Commutative Property true for repeated groups situations? Why or why not?

_____

_____

Class Activity

► Solve Array Problems

Make a math drawing for each problem and then solve.

Show your work.

18. Avi arranged her bottle cap collection into an array. The array had 4 rows with 9 bottle caps in each row. How many bottle caps are in her collection?

_____

19. On one wall of an art gallery, photographs were arranged in 2 rows with 7 photographs in each row. How many total photographs were on the wall?

_____

On a separate sheet of paper, write the answers to exercises 20–22.

20. In Lesson 1, you explored the relationship between division and multiplication. You saw that dividing means finding an unknown factor. Use this idea to explain what division is in an array situation.

► Write Division Problems

21. Write and solve two division word problems that are related to the multiplication word problem in problem 18.

22. Write and solve two division word problems that are related to the multiplication word problem in problem 19.

Name _____ **Date** _____

Class Activity

▶ **Checkup A: 2s, 5s, 9s, 10s**

1. $3 \times 2 =$ ___	19. $9 \times 5 =$ ___	37. $4 / 2 =$ ___	55. $2\overline{)6}$
2. $1 \cdot 5 =$ ___	20. $2 \times 2 =$ ___	38. $\frac{5}{5} =$ ___	56. $10 \div 5 =$ ___
3. $8 * 5 =$ ___	21. $5 * 3 =$ ___	39. $8 \div 2 =$ ___	57. $9\overline{)27}$
4. $9 \times 3 =$ ___	22. $10 \times 2 =$ ___	40. $9 \div 9 =$ ___	58. $40 \div 5 =$ ___
5. $5 \cdot 2 =$ ___	23. $5 \cdot 5 =$ ___	41. $50 / 5 =$ ___	59. $18 / 9 =$ ___
6. $9 * 9 =$ ___	24. $1 * 9 =$ ___	42. $2\overline{)20}$	60. $2 \div 2 =$ ___
7. $8 \times 2 =$ ___	25. $8 * 9 =$ ___	43. $54 \div 9 =$ ___	61. $36 / 9 =$ ___
8. $10 \cdot 4 =$ ___	26. $2 * 4 =$ ___	44. $10\overline{)10}$	62. $16 \div 2 =$ ___
9. $7 * 5 =$ ___	27. $5 \cdot 10 =$ ___	45. $\frac{10}{2} =$ ___	63. $5\overline{)15}$
10. $1 \times 10 =$ ___	28. $4 \times 9 =$ ___	46. $81 / 9 =$ ___	64. $63 / 9 =$ ___
11. $10 \cdot 6 =$ ___	29. $7 \cdot 2 =$ ___	47. $20 \div 10 =$ ___	65. $90 \div 9 =$ ___
12. $5 * 4 =$ ___	30. $10 * 3 =$ ___	48. $\frac{70}{10} =$ ___	66. $12 / 2 =$ ___
13. $9 \times 7 =$ ___	31. $7 \times 10 =$ ___	49. $5\overline{)30}$	67. $35 \div 5 =$ ___
14. $5 \cdot 6 =$ ___	32. $9 * 6 =$ ___	50. $80 / 10 =$ ___	68. $100 / 10 =$ ___
15. $2 * 1 =$ ___	33. $2 * 9 =$ ___	51. $\frac{45}{9} =$ ___	69. $\frac{45}{5} =$ ___
16. $6 \times 9 =$ ___	34. $10 \cdot 9 =$ ___	52. $20 / 5 =$ ___	70. $18 / 2 =$ ___
17. $10 \cdot 8 =$ ___	35. $10 \times 10 =$ ___	53. $2\overline{)14}$	71. $9\overline{)72}$
18. $2 * 6 =$ ___	36. $7 * 9 =$ ___	54. $60 \div 10 =$ ___	72. $25 \div 5 =$ ___

▶ Play a Game

Play *Quotient Match* with your partner.

Rules for *Quotient Match*

Number of players: 2 or 3
What you will need: Product Cards: 2s, 5s, 9s

1. Shuffle the cards. Put the cards, division side up, on the table in 6 rows of 4.

2. Players take turns. On each turn, a player chooses three cards that he or she thinks have the same quotient and turns them over.

3. If all three cards do have the same quotient the player takes them. If not, the player turns them back over so the division side is up.

4. Play continues until no cards remain.

5. The player with the most cards wins.

2×2

$2 \cdot 3$

Hint:
What is $3 \cdot 2$?

$2 * 4$

Hint:
What is $4 * 2$?

2×5

Hint:
What is 5×2?

2×6

Hint:
What is 6×2?

$2 \cdot 7$

Hint:
What is $7 \cdot 2$?

$2 * 8$

Hint:
What is $8 * 2$?

2×9

Hint:
What is 9×2?

5×2

Hint:
What is 2×5?

$5 \cdot 3$

Hint:
What is $3 \cdot 5$?

$5 * 4$

Hint:
What is $4 * 5$?

5×5

5×6

Hint:
What is 6×5?

$5 \cdot 7$

Hint:
What is $7 \cdot 5$?

$5 * 8$

Hint:
What is $8 * 5$?

5×9

Hint:
What is 9×5?

Product Cards: 2s, 5s, 9s

$2 \overline{)10}$

Hint: What is
$\square \times 2 = 10$?

$2 \overline{)8}$

Hint: What is
$\square \times 2 = 8$?

$2 \overline{)6}$

Hint: What is
$\square \times 2 = 6$?

$2 \overline{)4}$

Hint: What is
$\square \times 2 = 4$?

$2 \overline{)18}$

Hint: What is
$\square \times 2 = 18$?

$2 \overline{)16}$

Hint: What is
$\square \times 2 = 16$?

$2 \overline{)14}$

Hint: What is
$\square \times 2 = 14$?

$2 \overline{)12}$

Hint: What is
$\square \times 2 = 12$?

$5 \overline{)25}$

Hint: What is
$\square \times 5 = 25$?

$5 \overline{)20}$

Hint: What is
$\square \times 5 = 20$?

$5 \overline{)15}$

Hint: What is
$\square \times 5 = 15$?

$5 \overline{)10}$

Hint: What is
$\square \times 5 = 10$?

$5 \overline{)45}$

Hint: What is
$\square \times 5 = 45$?

$5 \overline{)40}$

Hint: What is
$\square \times 5 = 40$?

$5 \overline{)35}$

Hint: What is
$\square \times 5 = 35$?

$5 \overline{)30}$

Hint: What is
$\square \times 5 = 30$?

Product Cards: 2s, 5s, 9s

9×2

Hint:
What is 2×9?

$9 \cdot 3$

Hint:
What is $3 \cdot 9$?

$9 * 4$

Hint:
What is $4 * 9$?

9×5

Hint:
What is 5×9?

9×6

Hint:
What is 6×9?

$9 \cdot 7$

Hint:
What is $7 \cdot 9$?

$9 * 8$

Hint:
What is $8 * 9$?

9×9

$\times$

$\cdot$

$*$

$\times$

$\times$

$\cdot$

$*$

$\times$

You can write any numbers on the last 8 cards. Use them to practice difficult problems or if you lose a card.

Product Cards: 2s, 5s, 9s

$9\overline{)45}$

Hint: What is
☐ × 9 = 45?

$9\overline{)36}$

Hint: What is
☐ × 9 = 36?

$9\overline{)27}$

Hint: What is
☐ × 9 = 27?

$9\overline{)18}$

Hint: What is
☐ × 9 = 18?

$9\overline{)81}$

Hint: What is
☐ × 9 = 81?

$9\overline{)72}$

Hint: What is
☐ × 9 = 72?

$9\overline{)63}$

Hint: What is
☐ × 9 = 63?

$9\overline{)54}$

Hint: What is
☐ × 9 = 54?

You can write any numbers on the last 8 cards. Use them to practice difficult problems or if you lose a card.

Product Cards: 2s, 5s, 9s

Class Activity

Name _____ **Date** _____

▶ Solve Word Problems

Solve each problem.

Show your work.

1. Ben arranged his soccer trophies into 3 equal rows. If he has 12 trophies, how many trophies are in each row?

   _____

2. How many sides do 8 triangles have altogether?

   _____

3. For the yearbook photo, the science club stood in 3 rows with 5 students in each row. How many students were in the picture?

   _____

4. Tickets to the school play cost $3 each. Mr. Cortez spent $27 on tickets. How many tickets did he buy?

   _____

5. Jess solved 21 multiplication problems. If the problems were arranged in rows of 3, how many rows of problems did Jess solve?

   _____

6. Last year, 6 sets of triplets were born at Watertown hospital. During this time, how many total triplets were born at the hospital?

   _____

Class Activity

Vocabulary

Pictograph

▶ Pictographs

A **pictograph** is a graph that uses pictures to show data. The pictograph below shows the number of CDs of each type in Kyle's collection.

7. How many jazz CDs does Kyle have?

_____

8. How many hip hop CDs does Kyle have?

_____

Kyle's CDs

Type	Number of CDs
Jazz	🎵 🎵 🎵 🎵 🎵
Hip Hop	🎵 🎵 🎵 🎵 🎵 🎵 🎵 🎵
Rock	🎵 🎵 🎵
Classical	🎵 🎵

🎵 = 2 CDs

9. In all, how many jazz and classical CDs does Kyle have?

_____

10. How many more hip hop CDs than rock CDs does Kyle have?

_____

The pictograph below shows the numbers of pizzas of different sizes served last night at the Leaning Tower pizzeria.

11. How many medium pizzas did the restaurant serve?

_____

12. How many large pizzas did the restaurant serve?

_____

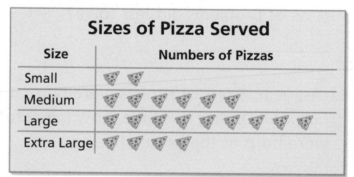

Sizes of Pizza Served

Size	Numbers of Pizzas
Small	🍕 🍕
Medium	🍕 🍕 🍕 🍕 🍕 🍕
Large	🍕 🍕 🍕 🍕 🍕 🍕 🍕 🍕 🍕
Extra Large	🍕 🍕 🍕 🍕

🍕 = 5 Pizzas

13. How many small and medium pizzas did the restaurant serve altogether? _____

▶ Equal-Shares Drawings

Complete each **Equal-Shares Drawing**. Then tell whether
the number in the box is a factor or the product.

1.   21

$3 \times$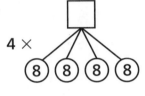

_____

2.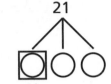

$2 \times$

_____

3.   20

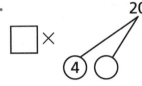

_____

4.

$4 \times$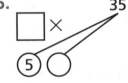

_____

5.   35

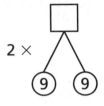

_____

6.   18

$6 \times$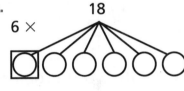

_____

7. Make up word problems for the drawings in exercises 3
and 4.

_____

_____

_____

_____

_____

_____

_____

_____

_____

_____

_____

▶ **Fast Arrays**

Complete each Fast Array.

8.
8
3 ○○○○○○○○
□

9.
9
□ 45 ○○○○○○○○○

10.
□
2 14

11.
5
□ 40 ○○○○○

12.
□
6 24

13.
8
○○○○○○○○
9 □

14. Write word problems for the drawings in exercises 8 and 12.

_____

_____

_____

_____

_____

_____

_____

_____

_____

_____

_____

_____

Multiply and Divide With 4

Class Activity

▶ Represent Multiplication With 1 and 0

Make a drawing to fit each description. Then write a multiplication equation to represent the total number of marbles.

1. 1 bag of 5 marbles

_____

2. 5 bags of 1 marble

_____

3. 0 bags of 5 marbles

_____

4. 5 bags of 0 marbles

_____

▶ Practice Multiplying 1 and 0

Find the product.

5. $1 \times 8 =$ _____

6. $9 \times 1 =$ _____

7. $0 \times 6 =$ _____

8. $7 \times 0 =$ _____

9. $1 \times 6 =$ _____

10. $4 \times 1 =$ _____

11. $0 \times 4 =$ _____

12. $3 \times 0 =$ _____

13. $1 \times 3 =$ _____

14. $7 \times 1 =$ _____

15. $0 \times 2 =$ _____

16. $8 \times 0 =$ _____

Name _____ **Date** _____

Class Activity

▶ Divide with 1

Draw a picture and write an equation to represent each situation.

17. 5 bagels are shared equally by 5 people.

18. 5 bagels are eaten by 1 person.

_____   _____

Look back at exercises 17 and 18. Replace each 5 with 4:

4 bagels shared by 4 people   4 bagels eaten by 1 person

$4 \div 4 = 1$ $4 \div 1 = 4$

19. Describe what you discovered. Can you make any general statements based on your discoveries?

_____

_____

▶ Practice Dividing with 1

Find the quotient.

20. $6 \div 1 =$ _____

21. $8 \div 8 =$ _____

22. $9 \div 1 =$ _____

23. $3 \div 3 =$ _____

24. $2 \div 1 =$ _____

25. $1 \div 1 =$ _____

26. $5 \div 1 =$ _____

27. $4 \div 4 =$ _____

28. $7 \div 1 =$ _____

Multiply and Divide With 1 and 0

Class Activity

▶ Divide with 0

29. If 0 bagels are shared equally by 5 people, what is each person's share? _____

30. Write a division equation to show the situation.

_____

31. Would you get the same answer if the 0 bagels were shared by a different number of people? _____

32. Can you make a general statement about dividing 0 things into any number of groups?

_____

33. Is it possible to divide 5 bagels among 0 people? Why or why not?

_____

_____

34. Rewrite the division problem $5 \div 0 =$ ___ as a multiplication problem. _____

35. Can you find a factor that makes the multiplication equation true? Why or why not?

_____

_____

▶ Mixed Practice with 1 and 0

Find the product or quotient.

36. $0 \times 8 =$ _____

37. $5 \div 5 =$ _____

38. $1 \times 9 =$ _____

39. $8 \div 8 =$ _____

40. $6 \times 1 =$ _____

41. $3 \div 1 =$ _____

42. $0 \div 9 =$ _____

43. $0 \times 2 =$ _____

44. $0 \div 4 =$ _____

45. $0 \times 0 =$ _____

46. $7 \times 1 =$ _____

47. $4 \times 1 =$ _____

Class Activity

▶ Add and Multiply with 1 and 0

Solve each problem.

48. $5 + 0 = $ _____   49. $0 + 1 = $ _____   50. $7 + 0 = $ _____

51. $5 \times 0 = $ _____   52. $0 \times 1 = $ _____   53. $7 \times 0 = $ _____

54. Describe how you can remember the patterns for adding 0 and for multiplying by 0 so you won't get confused.

_____

_____

_____

_____

55. $5 + 1 = $ _____   56. $1 + 2 = $ _____   57. $7 + 1 = $ _____

58. $5 \times 1 = $ _____   59. $1 \times 2 = $ _____   60. $7 \times 1 = $ _____

61. Describe how you can remember the pattern for adding 1 and for multiplying by 1 so you won't get confused.

_____

_____

_____

_____

62. Circle the two problems with the same answer.

   $6 + 0$ $6 + 1$ 6×0 6×1

Name _____ **Date** _____

Class Activity

► **Checkup B: 2s, 5s, 9s, 3s, 4s, 1s, 0s**

1. $5 * 3 =$ ___

2. $1 \cdot 5 =$ ___

3. $9 \times 5 =$ ___

4. $9 \times 3 =$ ___

5. $4 \cdot 8 =$ ___

6. $8 * 3 =$ ___

7. $8 \times 2 =$ ___

8. $10 \cdot 4 =$ ___

9. $7 * 5 =$ ___

10. $1 \times 10 =$ ___

11. $81 / 9 =$ ___

12. $5 * 4 =$ ___

13. $9 \times 7 =$ ___

14. $5 \cdot 6 =$ ___

15. $7 * 4 =$ ___

16. $6 \times 9 =$ ___

17. $10 \cdot 8 =$ ___

18. $2 * 6 =$ ___

19. $2\overline{)6}$

20. $10 \div 5 =$ ___

21. $4 / 2 =$ ___

22. $40 \div 5 =$ ___

23. $18 / 9 =$ ___

24. $21 \div 7 =$ ___

25. $36 / 9 =$ ___

26. $16 \div 2 =$ ___

27. $5\overline{)15}$

28. $90 \div 9 =$ ___

29. $35 \div 5 =$ ___

30. $0 / 10 =$ ___

31. $\frac{45}{5} =$ ___

32. $18 / 2 =$ ___

33. $9\overline{)72}$

34. $25 \div 5 =$ ___

35. $63 / 9 =$ ___

36. $12 / 2 =$ ___

37. $9\overline{)27}$

38. $\frac{24}{6} =$ ___

39. $8 \div 2 =$ ___

40. $9 \div 9 =$ ___

41. $50 / 5 =$ ___

42. $2\overline{)20}$

43. $54 \div 9 =$ ___

44. $10\overline{)10}$

45. $\frac{15}{3} =$ ___

46. $10 \cdot 6 =$ ___

47. $20 \div 10 =$ ___

48. $\frac{70}{10} =$ ___

49. $5\overline{)30}$

50. $80 / 10 =$ ___

51. $\frac{72}{9} =$ ___

52. $20 / 5 =$ ___

53. $2\overline{)14}$

54. $60 \div 10 =$ ___

55. $8 * 5 =$ ___

56. $4 \times 3 =$ ___

57. $3 \times 2 =$ ___

58. $8 \times 3 =$ ___

59. $3 \cdot 3 =$ ___

60. $7 * 3 =$ ___

61. $0 * 9 =$ ___

62. $2 * 4 =$ ___

63. $5 \cdot 10 =$ ___

64. $4 \times 9 =$ ___

65. $7 \cdot 2 =$ ___

66. $10 * 3 =$ ___

67. $7 \times 10 =$ ___

68. $3 * 6 =$ ___

69. $4 * 4 =$ ___

70. $2 \cdot 0 =$ ___

71. $7 * 4 =$ ___

72. $10 \times 10 =$ ___

Class Activity

Name _____

Date _____

▶ **Play a Game**

Play *High Card Wins* with your partner.

Rules for *High Card Wins*

Number of players: 2
What you will need: Product Cards: 2s, 3s, 4s, 5s, 9s

1. Shuffle the cards. Deal all the cards evenly between the two players.

2. Players put their stacks in front of them, multiplication side up.

3. Each player takes the top card from his or her stack and puts it multiplication side up in the center of the table.

4. Each player says the answer and then turns the card over to check. Then do one of the following:

   • If one player says the wrong answer, the other player takes both cards and puts them at the bottom of his or her pile.
   • If both players say the wrong answer, both players take back their cards and put them at the bottom of their piles.
   • If both players say the correct answer, the player with the higher product takes both cards and puts them at the bottom of his or her pile. If the products are the same, the players set the cards aside and play another round. The winner of the next round takes all the cards.

5. Play continues until one player has all the cards.

Fluency Day: 2s, 3s, 4s, 5s, 9s, and 10s

3×2	$3 \cdot 3$	$3 * 4$	3×5
Hint: What is 2×3?		**Hint:** What is $4 * 3$?	**Hint:** What is 5×3?

3×6	$3 \cdot 7$	$3 * 8$	3×9
Hint: What is 6×3?	**Hint:** What is $7 \cdot 3$?	**Hint:** What is $8 * 3$?	**Hint:** What is 9×3?

4×2	$4 \cdot 3$	$4 * 4$	4×5
Hint: What is 2×4?	**Hint:** What is $3 \cdot 4$?		**Hint:** What is 5×4?

4×6	$4 \cdot 7$	$4 * 8$	4×9
Hint: What is 6×4?	**Hint:** What is $7 \cdot 4$?	**Hint:** What is $8 * 4$?	**Hint:** What is 9×4?

$3\overline{)15}$

Hint: What is
$\square \times 3 = 15$?

$3\overline{)12}$

Hint: What is
$\square \times 3 = 12$?

$3\overline{)9}$

Hint: What is
$\square \times 3 = 9$?

$3\overline{)6}$

Hint: What is
$\square \times 3 = 6$?

$3\overline{)27}$

Hint: What is
$\square \times 3 = 27$?

$3\overline{)24}$

Hint: What is
$\square \times 3 = 24$?

$3\overline{)21}$

Hint: What is
$\square \times 3 = 21$?

$3\overline{)18}$

Hint: What is
$\square \times 3 = 18$?

$4\overline{)20}$

Hint: What is
$\square \times 4 = 20$?

$4\overline{)16}$

Hint: What is
$\square \times 4 = 16$?

$4\overline{)12}$

Hint: What is
$\square \times 4 = 12$?

$4\overline{)8}$

Hint: What is
$\square \times 4 = 8$?

$4\overline{)36}$

Hint: What is
$\square \times 4 = 36$?

$4\overline{)32}$

Hint: What is
$\square \times 4 = 32$?

$4\overline{)28}$

Hint: What is
$\square \times 4 = 28$?

$4\overline{)24}$

Hint: What is
$\square \times 4 = 24$?

Product Cards: 3s, 4s

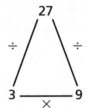

Class Activity

Name _____ **Date** _____

Vocabulary
Factor Triangle
Fast Array

► **Write Equations from a Factor Triangle**

1. Write eight equations based on this **Factor Triangle**.

_____ _____

_____ _____

_____ _____

_____ _____

► **Write Equations from a Fast Array**

2. Write eight equations based on this **Fast Array**.

```
      4
   • • • •
   •
7  • 28
   •
   •
   •
```

_____ _____

_____ _____

_____ _____

_____ _____

3. Draw a Factor Triangle and a Fast Array. Then write the other 7 equations.

Factor Triangle   Fast Array

$4 \times 6 = 24$ _____

_____ _____

_____ _____

_____ _____

▶ The Relationship Between Multiplication and Division

4. Write your ideas about how multiplication and division
are related.

_____

_____

_____

_____

_____

_____

_____

_____

_____

5. Explain how you can start with one multiplication or
division equation and then write seven other equations.

_____

_____

_____

_____

_____

_____

_____

_____

$7\overline{)3}$	$7\overline{)4}$	$6\overline{)0}$	$1\overline{)6}$	$1\overline{)3}$	$8\overline{)0}$
$4\overline{)2}$	$1\overline{)8}$	$6\overline{)1}$	$3\overline{)6}$	$2\overline{)4}$	$4\overline{)1}$
$5\overline{)3}$	$6\overline{)4}$	$10\overline{)0}$	$4\overline{)10}$	$5\overline{)0}$	$9\overline{)3}$
$3\overline{)1}$	$2\overline{)3}$	$5\overline{)4}$	$2\overline{)0}$	$10\overline{)4}$	$3\overline{)7}$
$4\overline{)0}$	$1\overline{)4}$	$3\overline{)8}$	$4\overline{)3}$	$3\overline{)2}$	$6\overline{)3}$
$1\overline{)2}$	$1\overline{)0}$	$9\overline{)4}$	$1\overline{)7}$	$8\overline{)1}$	$3\overline{)3}$
$4\overline{)5}$	$10\overline{)3}$	$4\overline{)7}$	$9\overline{)0}$	$4\overline{)9}$	$8\overline{)3}$
$3\overline{)4}$	$4\overline{)6}$	$1\overline{)5}$	$2\overline{)1}$	$3\overline{)9}$	$4\overline{)4}$
$9\overline{)1}$	$5\overline{)1}$	$3\overline{)5}$	$1\overline{)9}$	$3\overline{)0}$	$1\overline{)10}$
$7\overline{)0}$	$3\overline{)10}$	$7\overline{)1}$	$8\overline{)4}$	$10\overline{)1}$	$4\overline{)8}$

10)30	1)8	1)0	5)15	1)1	4)16
4)32	4)0	3)3	1)10	8)24	3)9
9)27	3)30	1)5	3)15	5)0	6)0
5)20	5)5	10)40	4)12	7)7	4)4
9)0	1)4	4)8	2)2	4)36	8)8
2)6	3)21	8)32	8)0	2)8	6)18
4)24	1)6	3)12	1)3	7)21	3)6
3)0	9)9	10)0	3)27	9)36	4)40
10)10	4)28	7)28	1)9	3)24	1)7
3)18	7)0	6)24	4)20	2)0	6)6

Class Write-On Sheet 1B

$$7\overline{)21}\quad 3$$
$$7\overline{)28}\quad 4$$
$$6\overline{)0}\quad 0$$
$$1\overline{)6}\quad 6$$
$$1\overline{)3}\quad 3$$
$$8\overline{)0}\quad 0$$

$$4\overline{)8}\quad 2$$
$$1\overline{)8}\quad 8$$
$$6\overline{)6}\quad 1$$
$$3\overline{)18}\quad 6$$
$$2\overline{)8}\quad 4$$
$$4\overline{)4}\quad 1$$

$$5\overline{)15}\quad 3$$
$$6\overline{)24}\quad 4$$
$$10\overline{)0}\quad 0$$
$$4\overline{)40}\quad 10$$
$$5\overline{)0}\quad 0$$
$$9\overline{)27}\quad 3$$

$$3\overline{)3}\quad 1$$
$$2\overline{)6}\quad 3$$
$$5\overline{)20}\quad 4$$
$$2\overline{)0}\quad 0$$
$$10\overline{)40}\quad 4$$
$$3\overline{)21}\quad 7$$

$$4\overline{)0}\quad 0$$
$$1\overline{)4}\quad 4$$
$$3\overline{)24}\quad 8$$
$$4\overline{)12}\quad 3$$
$$3\overline{)6}\quad 2$$
$$6\overline{)18}\quad 3$$

$$1\overline{)2}\quad 2$$
$$1\overline{)0}\quad 0$$
$$9\overline{)36}\quad 4$$
$$1\overline{)7}\quad 7$$
$$8\overline{)8}\quad 1$$
$$3\overline{)9}\quad 3$$

$$4\overline{)20}\quad 5$$
$$10\overline{)30}\quad 3$$
$$4\overline{)28}\quad 7$$
$$9\overline{)0}\quad 0$$
$$4\overline{)36}\quad 9$$
$$8\overline{)24}\quad 3$$

$$3\overline{)12}\quad 4$$
$$4\overline{)24}\quad 6$$
$$1\overline{)5}\quad 5$$
$$2\overline{)2}\quad 1$$
$$3\overline{)27}\quad 9$$
$$4\overline{)16}\quad 4$$

$$9\overline{)9}\quad 1$$
$$5\overline{)5}\quad 1$$
$$3\overline{)15}\quad 5$$
$$1\overline{)9}\quad 9$$
$$3\overline{)0}\quad 0$$
$$1\overline{)10}\quad 10$$

$$7\overline{)0}\quad 0$$
$$3\overline{)30}\quad 10$$
$$7\overline{)7}\quad 1$$
$$8\overline{)32}\quad 4$$
$$10\overline{)10}\quad 1$$
$$4\overline{)32}\quad 8$$

$10\overline{)30}$ → 3	$1\overline{)8}$ → 8	$1\overline{)0}$ → 0	$5\overline{)15}$ → 3	$1\overline{)1}$ → 1	$4\overline{)16}$ → 4
$4\overline{)32}$ → 8	$4\overline{)0}$ → 0	$3\overline{)3}$ → 1	$1\overline{)10}$ → 10	$8\overline{)24}$ → 3	$3\overline{)9}$ → 3
$9\overline{)27}$ → 3	$3\overline{)30}$ → 10	$1\overline{)5}$ → 5	$3\overline{)15}$ → 5	$5\overline{)0}$ → 0	$6\overline{)0}$ → 0
$5\overline{)20}$ → 4	$5\overline{)5}$ → 1	$10\overline{)40}$ → 4	$4\overline{)12}$ → 3	$7\overline{)7}$ → 1	$4\overline{)4}$ → 1
$9\overline{)0}$ → 0	$1\overline{)4}$ → 4	$4\overline{)8}$ → 2	$2\overline{)2}$ → 1	$4\overline{)36}$ → 9	$8\overline{)8}$ → 1
$2\overline{)6}$ → 3	$3\overline{)21}$ → 7	$8\overline{)32}$ → 4	$8\overline{)0}$ → 0	$2\overline{)8}$ → 4	$6\overline{)18}$ → 3
$4\overline{)24}$ → 6	$1\overline{)6}$ → 6	$3\overline{)12}$ → 4	$1\overline{)3}$ → 3	$7\overline{)21}$ → 3	$3\overline{)6}$ → 2
$3\overline{)0}$ → 0	$9\overline{)9}$ → 1	$10\overline{)0}$ → 0	$3\overline{)27}$ → 9	$9\overline{)36}$ → 4	$4\overline{)40}$ → 10
$10\overline{)10}$ → 1	$4\overline{)28}$ → 7	$7\overline{)28}$ → 4	$1\overline{)9}$ → 9	$3\overline{)24}$ → 8	$1\overline{)7}$ → 7
$3\overline{)18}$ → 6	$7\overline{)0}$ → 0	$6\overline{)24}$ → 4	$4\overline{)20}$ → 5	$2\overline{)0}$ → 0	$6\overline{)6}$ → 1

Class Check Sheet 1B

Class Activity

▶ Identify the Problem Type

Identify the type for each problem. Choose from this list. (Write the letter, not the words.)

a. **Array** Multiplication
b. Array Division
c. **Repeated-Groups** Multiplication
d. Repeated-Groups Division with Unknown Group Size
e. Repeated-Groups Division with Unknown Multiplier (number of groups)

For each multiplication problem, write a multiplication equation. For each division problem, write both a division equation and a multiplication equation.

1. Latisha's uncle gave her 32 stamps and a new stamp book. The book has 8 pages, and she put the same number of stamps on each page. How many stamps did she put on each page?

   Problem type: _____   **Equation(s):** _____

2. A parking lot has 7 rows of parking spaces. Each row has 7 spaces. How many cars can park in the lot?

   Problem type: _____   **Equation(s):** _____

3. Janine planted 5 rows of roses. If she planted a total of 40 roses, how many did she plant in each row?

   Problem type: _____   **Equation(s):** _____

4. The produce market sells oranges in bags of 6. Santos bought 4 bags. How many oranges did he buy?

   Problem type: _____   **Equation(s):** _____

▶ Write Word Problems

5. **On the Back** Write two word problems of different types.

_____

_____

_____

_____

_____

_____

_____

_____

_____

_____

_____

_____

_____

_____

_____

_____

_____

_____

_____

_____

▶ Multiplication Strategies

These strategies will help you find 6×6:

| **Strategy 1:** Start with 5×6, and count by 6 from there:

$5 \times 6 = 30$, plus 6 more is 36.

So, $6 \times 6 = 36$. | **Strategy 2:** Double a 3s multiplication:

6×6 is twice 6×3, which is 18.

So, $6 \times 6 = 18 + 18 = 36$. | **Strategy 3:** Combine two multiplications you know:

$4 \times 6 = 24$ 4 sixes are 24
$2 \times 6 = 12$ 2 sixes are 12
$6 \times 6 = 36$ 6 sixes are 36 |

1. Make a Fast Array or an Equal-Shares Drawing to show why Strategy 3 works.

2. Choose one of the strategies above. Explain how you could use it to find 7×6.

_____

_____

_____

3. Choose one of the other strategies. Explain how you could use it to find 8×6.

_____

_____

_____

Name _____ **Date** _____

Going Further

Vocabulary

function
rule

▶ Function Tables

The numbers in each column of a horizontal function table share the same relationship.

What do you do to the top number to get the bottom number? Describe in words and write an equation using the letters.

Yards	y	1	2	3	4	5	6	7	10	100
Feet	f	3	6	9	12	15				

The relationship shared by yards and feet is an example of a **function**.

For each table below, decide what to do to the top number. Write a **rule** in words and write an equation. Then complete the table.

1.

Birds	b	1	2	3	4	5	6	7	10	100
Wings	w	2	4	6	8	10				

2.

Dollars	d	1	2	3	4	5	6	7	10	100
Dimes	m	10	20	30	40	50				

3.

Starfish	s	0	2	4	5	8	9	12	10	100
Arms	a	0	10	20	25	40				

Multiply and Divide With 6

Dear Family,

As your child continues to learn the basics of multiplication and division, he or she will bring home a variety of practice materials that are designed to help build fluency.

- **Target** This is a shaded overlay with a transparent L-shape and a circle. They are used together with students' multiplication tables. When the Target is placed over a multiplication table, the ends of the L show the factors, and the Target circle shows the product. Covering the product provides multiplication practice. Covering one end of the L provides division practice.

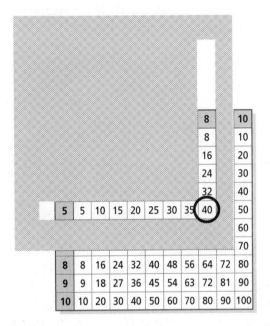

- **Write-On and Check Sheets** Students place Write-On Sheets in sheet protectors and try to solve various multiplication and division problems with a dry-erase marker. Students check their answers using Check Sheets.

- **Product Cards** Students first decide which side of each card will be facing up in their stack—multiplication or division. Students should choose the operation that is most difficult for them. After the student solves the problem mentally, he or she turns the card over to check his or her answer. Students should sort their Product Cards into *Fast, Slow,* and *Don't Know* piles.

Please provide a regular time and a quiet place for practice every night and keep the practice materials in a special place at home so your child does not lose them.

Sincerely,
Your child's teacher

Estimada familia:

A medida que aprendemos las reglas básicas de la multiplicación y la división, su niño llevará a casa una variedad de materiales de práctica que lo ayudarán a resolver estas operaciones con fluidez.

• **Objetivo** Es un acetato sombreado que tiene una zona transparente en forma de L y un círculo. Por lo general, se usa junto con las tablas de multiplicar de los estudiantes. Cuando el acetato se coloca sobre una tabla de multiplicar, los extremos de la L muestran los factores y el círculo muestra el producto. Se puede cubrir el producto para practicar la multiplicación. Se puede cubrir un extremo de la L para practicar la división.

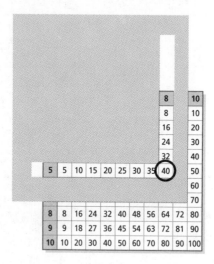

• **Hojas para escribir y comprobar** Los estudiantes colocan hojas para escribir sobre protectores de hojas y tratan de resolver varias operaciones de multiplicación y división con un marcador de agua. Los estudiantes comprueban las respuestas usando las Hojas para comprobar.

• **Tarjetas de productos** Los estudiantes deben decidir qué lado de cada tarjeta estará boca arriba en la pila; el de multiplicación o el de división. Es preferible que elijan la operación que les resulte más difícil. Una vez que el estudiante haya resuelto el problema mentalmente, dará vuelta a la tarjeta para verificar su respuesta. Los estudiantes deben clasificar sus Tarjetas de productos en tres grupos: *Rápido, Despacio* y *No sé*.

Por favor establezca un horario y un lugar tranquilo para que el niño practique cada noche y guarde los materiales en un lugar específico para que el niño no los pierda.

Atentamente,
El maestro de su niño

Multiply and Divide With 6

▶ Use Multiplication Strategies

Read the letter. Help the Puzzled Penguin by answering the question.

Dear Math Students:

Today I had to find 8 × 7. I didn't know the answer, but I figured it out by combining two multiplications I did know:

$$5 \times 3 = 15$$
$$3 \times 4 = 12$$
$$\overline{8 \times 7 = 27}$$

Is my answer right? If not, please help me understand why it is wrong.

Thank you,

Puzzled Penguin

_____

_____

_____

_____

_____

_____

_____

_____

_____

_____

► **Solve and Discuss**

Show your work.

Solve each problem.

1. Julian arranged his swimming trophies on the 8 shelves above his dresser. He put 7 trophies on each shelf. How many trophies does he have?

_____

2. Six students from Maile's class baked cakes for their school's cakewalk fundraiser. They each brought 6 cakes. How many cakes were there in all?

_____

3. Roberto has an orchard with 48 peach trees. They are planted in 6 rows. How many columns of peach trees are in his orchard?

_____

4. Kyle has 8 friends who would like to start an ant farm like his. He took 64 ants from his farm and divided them equally into 8 containers for his friends. How many ants will each friend receive?

_____

5. Frances decides to sell her model airplane collection at her family's yard sale. She arranges her model planes on a table. She puts them in 6 rows, with 7 planes in each row. How many planes does she have for sale?

_____

6. Tamara has just harvested the garlic she planted last fall. She has 49 heads of garlic. She plans to braid them into 7 equal bunches to use as gifts. How many heads of garlic will be in each bunch?

_____

Class Activity

Vocabulary
square array
square numbers

► Equations for Square Arrays

Write an equation to show the total number of dots in each square array.

1. _____

•

2. _____

3. _____

4. _____

5. _____

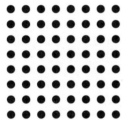

6. _____

7. _____

8. _____

9. _____

10. _____

The products in exercises 1–10 are **square numbers**. A square number is the product of a whole number and itself. So, if *n* is a whole number, *n* × *n* is a square number.

► Find a Pattern

11. **Challenge** Describe the pattern in the number of dots added from one square array to the next.

_____

_____

_____

Class Activity

▶ Patterns in the Multiplication Table

12. In the table, circle the product *n* × *n* for every value of *n* from 1 to 10. Then discuss patterns you see.

×	1	2	3	4	5	6	7	8	9	10
1	1	2	3	4	5	6	7	8	9	10
2	2	4	6	8	10	12	14	16	18	20
3	3	6	9	12	15	18	21	24	27	30
4	4	8	12	16	20	24	28	32	36	40
5	5	10	15	20	25	30	35	40	45	50
6	6	12	18	24	30	36	42	48	54	60
7	7	14	21	28	35	42	49	56	63	70
8	8	16	24	32	40	48	56	64	72	80
9	9	18	27	36	45	54	63	72	81	90
10	10	20	30	40	50	60	70	80	90	100

13. Discuss the patterns you see in each column of the table.

×	11	12
1	1 × 11 = **11**	1 × 12 = **12**
2	2 × 11 = **22**	2 × 12 = **24**
3	3 × 11 = **33**	3 × 12 = **36**
4	4 × 11 = **44**	4 × 12 = **48**
5	5 × 11 = **55**	5 × 12 = **60**
6	6 × 11 = **66**	6 × 12 = **72**
7	7 × 11 = **77**	7 × 12 = **84**
8	8 × 11 = **88**	8 × 12 = **96**
9	9 × 11 = **99**	9 × 12 = **108**
10	10 × 11 = **110**	10 × 12 = **120**

Square Numbers, 11s and 12s

Class Activity

Name _____ Date _____

► **Properties and Conjectures**

Vocabulary
Commutative Property of Multiplication
Identity Property of Multiplication

The **Commutative Property of Multiplication** states that you can switch the order of the factors without changing the product:

$$a \cdot b = b \cdot a \text{ for any numbers } a \text{ and } b$$

The **Identity Property of Multiplication** states that the product of 1 and any other number is that number:

$$1 \cdot n = n \text{ and } n \cdot 1 = n, \text{ for any number } n$$

---

1. Do you think there is a Commutative Property of Subtraction? That is, do you think $a - b = b - a$, for any numbers a and b? Test pairs of values to help you decide.

   _____

   _____

   _____

   _____

2. Do you think there is a Commutative Property of Division? That is, do you think $a \div b = b \div a$, for any numbers a and b? Test pairs of values to help you decide.

   _____

   _____

   _____

   _____

Use the Commutative Property of Multiplication to find the value of n.

3. $29 \times 8 = 8 \times n$

   _____

4. $n \times 49 = 49 \times 16$

   _____

5. $7 \times n = 36 \times 7$

   _____

▶ The Associative Property

6. How do these pictures show that $(3 \times 4) \times 2 = 3 \times (4 \times 2)$?

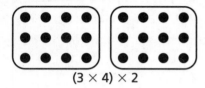

$(3 \times 4) \times 2$

$3 \times (4 \times 2)$

_____

_____

_____

Find both products in each problem. Show how you got your answers.

7. $(6 \times 2) \times 3$ and $6 \times (2 \times 3)$

_____

8. $(7 \times 5) \times 2$ and $7 \times (5 \times 2)$

_____

The **Associative Property** states that the product is the same no matter how the factors are grouped:

$$(a \cdot b) \cdot c = a \cdot (b \cdot c), \text{ for any numbers } a, b, \text{ and } c$$

▶ The Distributive Property

Here are two ways to find the number of dots in this array:

- **Method 1:** First, add the number of gray columns and the number of black columns to get the total number of columns. Then, multiply the total number of columns by the number of rows.

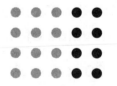

- **Method 2:** First, multiply to find the number of dots in each array. Then, add the results.

Notice that both methods give the same answer:
$4 \cdot (3 + 2) = (4 \cdot 3) + (4 \cdot 2)$.

Name _____ **Date** _____

Class Activity

▶ The Distributive Property (Continued)

9. Find the number of dots in this array by adding the number of gray rows and the number of black rows and then multiplying by the number of columns. Fill in the blanks below to show this.

   (__ + __) • __ = __ • __ = __

10. You can also find the number of dots in the gray array and the number of dots in the black array and then add the results. Fill in the blanks below to show this.

    __ • __ + __ • __ = __ + __ = __

11. Write a single equation showing that the two methods give the same answer.

    (__ + __) • __ = __ • __ + __ • __

The **Distributive Property** states that multiplication *distributes* over addition:

$$a \cdot (b + c) = a \cdot b + a \cdot c \text{ and } (b + c) \cdot a = b \cdot a + c \cdot a,$$
for any numbers *a*, *b*, and *c*

Use the Distributive Property to rewrite the expression so that it has only one multiplication and one addition.

12. 6 • 3 + 6 • 4   13. 2 × 7 + 8 × 7   14. 4 * 6 + 4 * 3

_____   _____   _____

Use the Distributive Property to rewrite the expression as the sum of two multiplications.

15. 8 • (2 + 4)   16. (5 + 4) • 6   17. 4 • (7 + 5)

_____   _____   _____

Name _____   **Date** _____

Going Further

▶ Order of Operations

When an expression contains more than one operation, its value will depend on the order in which the operations are performed. Mathematicians have developed a set of rules for simplifying expressions.

ORDER OF OPERATIONS

- Compute inside parentheses first.
- Multiply and divide from left to right.
- Add and subtract from left to right.

$(4 + 5) \times 3$

$9 \quad \times 3 = 27$

Do operations in parentheses first.

$4 + 5 \times 3$

$4 + \quad 15 \quad = 19$

Without parentheses, multiply before adding.

$12 \div 6 \div 2$

$2 \quad \div 2 = 1$

Divide from left to right.

$(2 \times 4) \times (6 \div 2)$

$8 \quad \times \quad 3 \quad = 24$

Do operations in parentheses first.

Simplify each expression.

1. $6 \times 4 - 4$

_____

2. $6 \times (4 - 4)$

_____

3. $8 + 2 \times 7$

_____

4. $(3 + 4) \times 6$

_____

5. $(6 \times 3) - (2 \times 5)$

_____

6. $2 \times (6 - 2) \times 5$

_____

7. $5 + 3 \times 4$

_____

8. $(3 + 4) \times (7 - 2)$

_____

9. $18 \div 6 \div 3$

_____

10. $3 \times (10 - 9)$

_____

11. $3 \times 10 - 9$

_____

12. $15 \div 3 + 5 \times 2$

_____

13. Write four numerical expressions using at least two different operations in each. Use parentheses in two of them. Then ask a partner to simplify all of them.

_____   _____

_____   _____

     Properties of Multiplication

Class Activity

▶ Target Practice A

×	1	2	3	5	4	8	6	9	10	7
4	4	8	12	20	16	32	24	36	40	28
1	1	2	3	5	4	8	6	9	10	7
5	5	10	15	25	20	40	30	45	50	35
2	2	4	6	10	8	16	12	18	20	14
3	3	6	9	15	12	24	18	27	30	21
10	10	20	30	50	40	80	60	90	100	70
6	6	12	18	30	24	48	36	54	60	42
9	9	18	27	45	36	72	54	81	90	63
8	8	16	24	40	32	64	48	72	80	56
7	7	14	21	35	28	56	42	63	70	49

×	4	6	7	8
1	4	6	7	8
2	8	12	14	16
3	12	18	21	24
4	16	24	28	32
5	20	30	35	40
6	24	36	42	48
7	28	42	49	56
8	32	48	56	64
9	36	54	63	72
10	40	60	70	80

×	9	4	8	7	6	7	9	6	8	4
6	54	24	48	42	36	42	54	36	48	24
7	63	28	56	49	42	49	63	42	56	28
4	36	16	32	28	24	28	36	24	32	16
9	81	36	72	63	54	63	81	54	72	36
8	72	32	64	56	48	56	72	48	64	32
6	54	24	48	42	36	42	54	36	48	24
9	81	36	72	63	54	63	81	54	72	36
8	72	32	64	56	48	56	72	48	64	32
7	63	28	56	49	42	49	63	42	56	28
4	36	16	32	28	24	28	36	24	32	16

×	4	6	7	8
3	12	18	21	24
2	8	12	14	16
5	20	30	35	40
1	4	6	7	8
4	16	24	28	32
8	32	48	56	64
10	40	60	70	80
7	28	42	49	56
6	24	36	42	48
9	36	54	63	72

► Target Practice B

×	2	6	8	5	10	9	4	7	3	1
7	14	42	56	35	70	63	28	49	21	7
8	16	48	64	40	80	72	32	56	24	8
4	8	24	32	20	40	36	16	28	12	4
9	18	54	72	45	90	81	36	63	27	9
6	12	36	48	30	60	54	24	42	18	6
4	8	24	32	20	40	36	16	28	12	4
6	12	36	48	30	60	54	24	42	18	6
9	18	54	72	45	90	81	36	63	27	9
7	14	42	56	35	70	63	28	49	21	7
8	16	48	64	40	80	72	32	56	24	8

×	6	9	8	7	4
7	42	63	56	49	28
8	48	72	64	56	32
4	24	36	32	28	16
3	18	27	24	21	12
6	36	54	48	42	24
10	60	90	80	70	40
5	30	45	40	35	20
1	6	9	8	7	4
9	54	81	72	63	36
2	12	18	16	14	8

×	7	4	9	6	8	7	9	4	8	6
4	28	16	36	24	32	28	36	16	32	24
7	49	28	63	42	56	49	63	28	56	42
6	42	24	54	36	48	42	54	24	48	36
9	63	36	81	54	72	63	81	36	72	54
8	56	32	72	48	64	56	72	32	64	48
9	63	36	81	54	72	63	81	36	72	54
6	42	24	54	36	48	42	54	24	48	36
8	56	32	72	48	64	56	72	32	64	48
7	49	28	63	42	56	49	63	28	56	42
4	28	16	36	24	32	28	36	16	32	24

×	6	7	8	4	9
7	42	49	56	28	63
8	48	56	64	32	72
4	24	28	32	16	36
9	54	63	72	36	81
6	36	42	48	24	54
8	48	56	64	32	72
4	24	28	32	16	36
9	54	63	72	36	81
7	42	49	56	28	63
6	36	42	48	24	54

6×2

Hint:
What is 2×6?
Copyright © Houghton Mifflin Company

$6 \cdot 3$

Hint:
What is $3 \cdot 6$?
Copyright © Houghton Mifflin Company

$6 * 4$

Hint:
What is $4 * 6$?
Copyright © Houghton Mifflin Company

6×5

Hint:
What is 5×6?
Copyright © Houghton Mifflin Company

6×6

Copyright © Houghton Mifflin Company

$6 \cdot 7$

Hint:
What is $7 \cdot 6$?
Copyright © Houghton Mifflin Company

$6 * 8$

Hint:
What is $8 * 6$?
Copyright © Houghton Mifflin Company

6×9

Hint:
What is 9×6?
Copyright © Houghton Mifflin Company

7×2

Hint:
What is 2×7?
Copyright © Houghton Mifflin Company

$7 \cdot 3$

Hint:
What is $3 \cdot 7$?
Copyright © Houghton Mifflin Company

$7 * 4$

Hint:
What is $4 * 7$?
Copyright © Houghton Mifflin Company

7×5

Hint:
What is 5×7?
Copyright © Houghton Mifflin Company

7×6

Hint:
What is 6×7?
Copyright © Houghton Mifflin Company

$7 \cdot 7$

Copyright © Houghton Mifflin Company

$7 * 8$

Hint:
What is $8 * 7$?
Copyright © Houghton Mifflin Company

7×9

Hint:
What is 9×7?
Copyright © Houghton Mifflin Company

$6\overline{)30}$

Hint: What is
$\square \times 6 = 30$?
Copyright © Houghton Mifflin Company

$6\overline{)24}$

Hint: What is
$\square \times 6 = 24$?
Copyright © Houghton Mifflin Company

$6\overline{)18}$

Hint: What is
$\square \times 6 = 18$?
Copyright © Houghton Mifflin Company

$6\overline{)12}$

Hint: What is
$\square \times 6 = 12$?
Copyright © Houghton Mifflin Company

$6\overline{)54}$

Hint: What is
$\square \times 6 = 54$?
Copyright © Houghton Mifflin Company

$6\overline{)48}$

Hint: What is
$\square \times 6 = 48$?
Copyright © Houghton Mifflin Company

$6\overline{)42}$

Hint: What is
$\square \times 6 = 42$?
Copyright © Houghton Mifflin Company

$6\overline{)36}$

Hint: What is
$\square \times 6 = 36$?
Copyright © Houghton Mifflin Company

$7\overline{)35}$

Hint: What is
$\square \times 7 = 35$?
Copyright © Houghton Mifflin Company

$7\overline{)28}$

Hint: What is
$\square \times 7 = 28$?
Copyright © Houghton Mifflin Company

$7\overline{)21}$

Hint: What is
$\square \times 7 = 21$?
Copyright © Houghton Mifflin Company

$7\overline{)14}$

Hint: What is
$\square \times 7 = 14$?
Copyright © Houghton Mifflin Company

$7\overline{)63}$

Hint: What is
$\square \times 7 = 63$?
Copyright © Houghton Mifflin Company

$7\overline{)56}$

Hint: What is
$\square \times 7 = 56$?
Copyright © Houghton Mifflin Company

$7\overline{)49}$

Hint: What is
$\square \times 7 = 49$?
Copyright © Houghton Mifflin Company

$7\overline{)42}$

Hint: What is
$\square \times 7 = 42$?
Copyright © Houghton Mifflin Company

Product Cards: 6s, 7s, 8s

8 × 2

Hint:
What is 2 × 8?

8 • 3

Hint:
What is 3 • 8?

8 * 4

Hint:
What is 4 * 8?

8 × 5

Hint:
What is 5 × 8?

8 × 6

Hint:
What is 6 × 8?

8 • 7

Hint:
What is 7 • 8?

8 * 8

8 × 9

Hint:
What is 9 × 8?

×

•

*

×

×

•

*

×

You can write any numbers on the last 8 cards. Use them to practice difficult problems or if you lose a card.

Product Cards: 6s, 7s, 8s

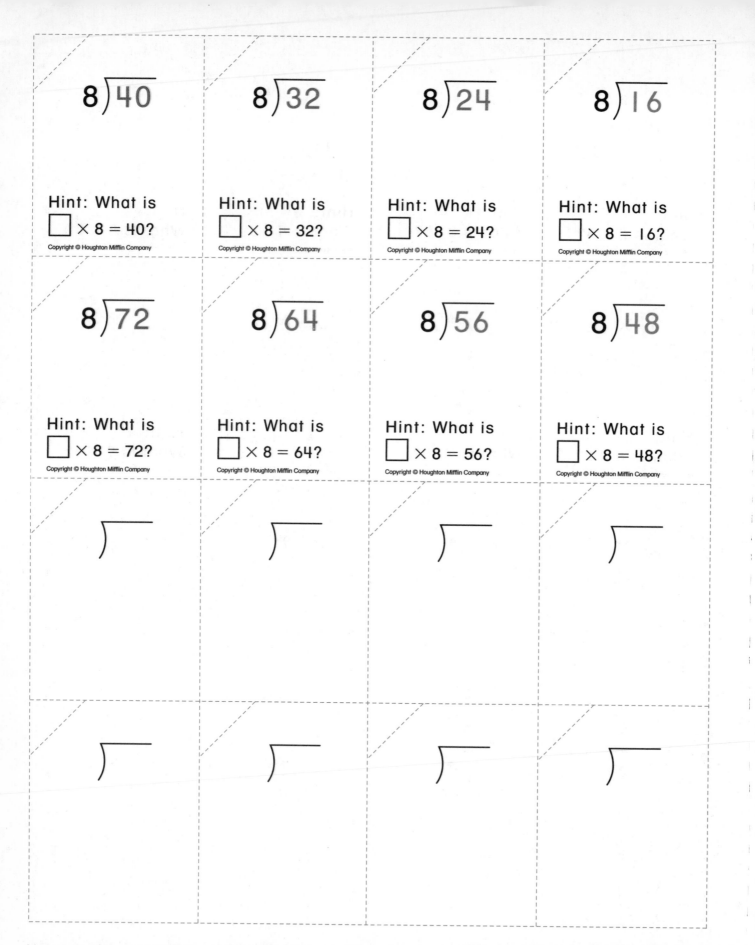

$8 \overline{)40}$

Hint: What is
$\square \times 8 = 40$?

Copyright © Houghton Mifflin Company

$8 \overline{)32}$

Hint: What is
$\square \times 8 = 32$?

Copyright © Houghton Mifflin Company

$8 \overline{)24}$

Hint: What is
$\square \times 8 = 24$?

Copyright © Houghton Mifflin Company

$8 \overline{)16}$

Hint: What is
$\square \times 8 = 16$?

Copyright © Houghton Mifflin Company

$8 \overline{)72}$

Hint: What is
$\square \times 8 = 72$?

Copyright © Houghton Mifflin Company

$8 \overline{)64}$

Hint: What is
$\square \times 8 = 64$?

Copyright © Houghton Mifflin Company

$8 \overline{)56}$

Hint: What is
$\square \times 8 = 56$?

Copyright © Houghton Mifflin Company

$8 \overline{)48}$

Hint: What is
$\square \times 8 = 48$?

Copyright © Houghton Mifflin Company

You can write any numbers on the last 8 cards. Use them to practice difficult problems or if you lose a card.

Product Cards: 6s, 7s, 8s

Name ______________________ Date ______________

▶ Practice with Factor Triangles

Fill in the unknown number in each Factor Triangle.

1.

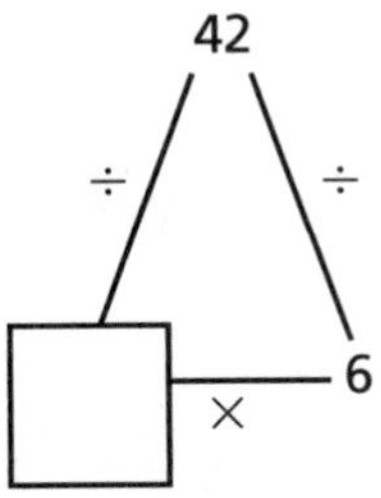

2.

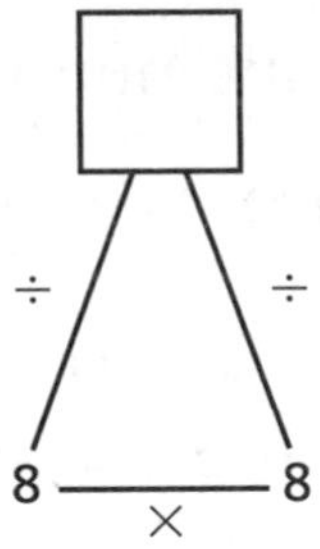

3.

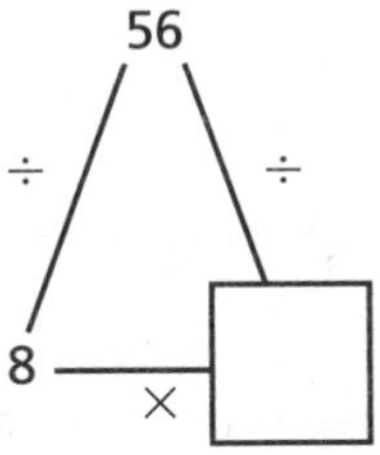

4.

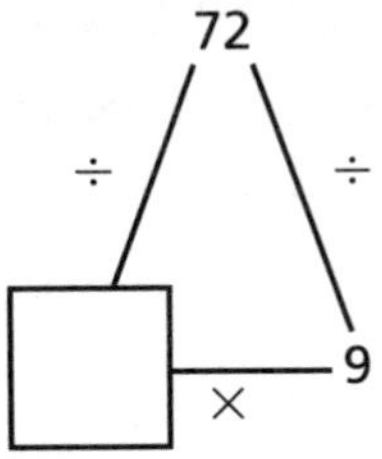

5.

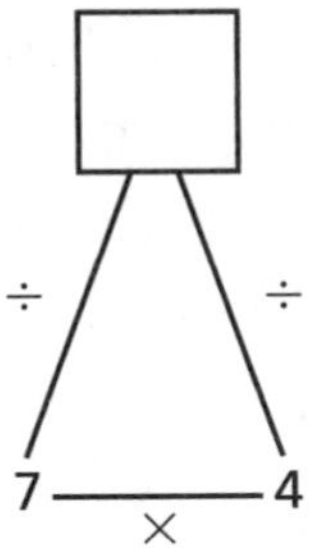

6.

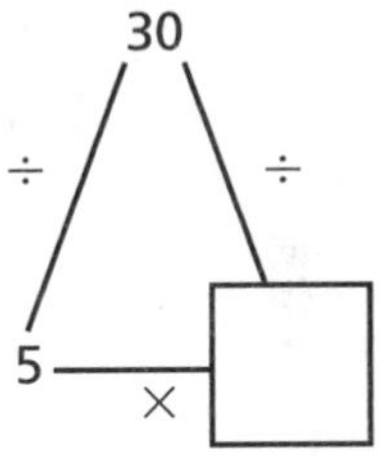

7.

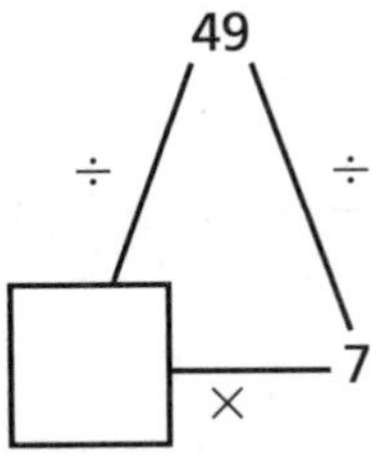

8.

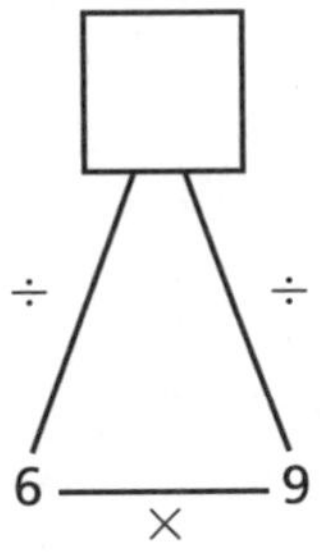

9.

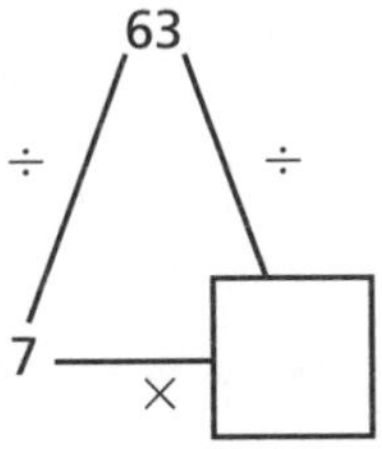

10.

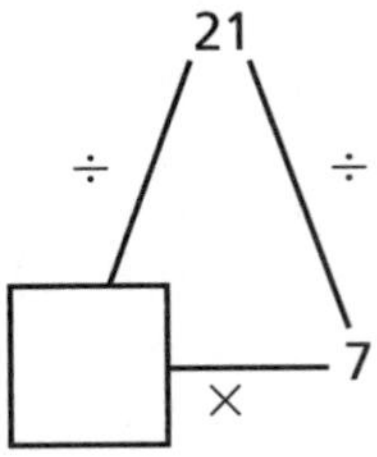

11.

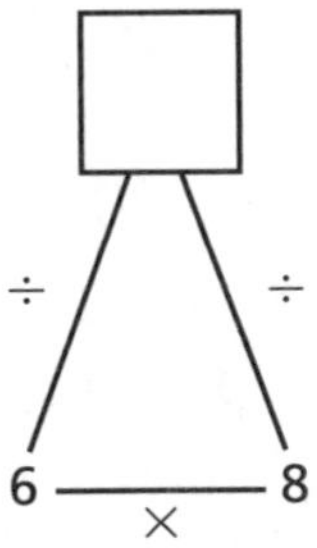

12.

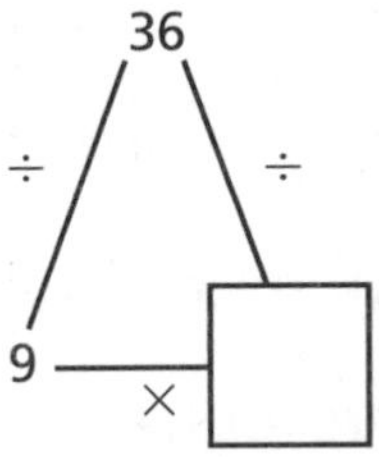

Going Further

Vocabulary
expression
number sentence
equation
inequality

▶ Expressions and Inequalities

In mathematics, an **expression** may use numbers, operations, and variables to represent an amount. All of these numerical expressions represent the number 6.

$1 + 2 + 3$ $10 - 4$ $12 \div 2$ 2×3 $2 \times (2 + 1)$

A **number sentence** describes how numbers or expressions are related to each other using the symbols $=$, $<$, or $>$. There are two kinds of number sentences.

An **equation** is a number sentence that uses an equals sign ($=$) to show that two expressions are equal.
 	
Example:
  $13 - 1 = 2 \times 6$
	An **inequality** is a number sentence that uses a $<$ or $>$ symbol to show that two expressions are not equal.
	
	Example:
	  $2 + 8 < 3 \times 4$

▶ Simplify and Compare

Write $<$, $>$, or $=$ to compare the expressions.

1. $5 + 8 \underline{\quad} 14 - 4$

2. $30 \div 5 \underline{\quad} 30 - 5$

3. $3 + 6 + 0 \underline{\quad} 5 \times 2$

4. $7 \underline{\quad} 4 \times 3$

5. $4 \times 5 \underline{\quad} 5 + 5 + 5$

6. $7 + 5 + 3 \underline{\quad} 3 \times 5$

7. $18 - 9 \underline{\quad} 20 \div 4$

8. $6 + 3 \underline{\quad} 3 \times 6$

9. $25 \underline{\quad} 2 \times 10$

10. $2 + 4 + 6 \underline{\quad} 15$

11. $20 + 5 \underline{\quad} 20 \div 5$

12. $1 \times 10 \underline{\quad} 1 \times 1 \times 0$

13. $4 + 0 + 6 \underline{\quad} 15 \times 1$

14. $6 \cdot 4 \underline{\quad} 2 \times (3 + 7)$

15. $3 \times 0 \underline{\quad} (4 + 2) - 5$

Write two equations and two inequalities.

_____   _____

_____   _____

Class Activity

Name   Date

▶ **Checkup C: 3s, 4s, 6s, 7s, 8s**

1. $8 \times 5 =$ ___

2. $7 \cdot 1 =$ ___

3. $4 * 8 =$ ___

4. $6 \times 2 =$ ___

5. $7 \cdot 7 =$ ___

6. $8 * 9 =$ ___

7. $4 \times 4 =$ ___

8. $8 \cdot 9 =$ ___

9. $4 * 4 =$ ___

10. $3 \times 8 =$ ___

11. $4 \cdot 9 =$ ___

12. $4 * 3 =$ ___

13. $8 \times 6 =$ ___

14. $7 \cdot 4 =$ ___

15. $7 * 8 =$ ___

16. $6 \times 4 =$ ___

17. $7 \cdot 3 =$ ___

18. $6 * 9 =$ ___

19. $4 \times 6 =$ ___

20. $7 \times 2 =$ ___

21. $6 * 3 =$ ___

22. $4 \times 7 =$ ___

23. $6 \cdot 10 =$ ___

24. $8 * 4 =$ ___

25. $7 * 6 =$ ___

26. $8 * 8 =$ ___

27. $4 \cdot 2 =$ ___

28. $8 \times 7 =$ ___

29. $6 \cdot 5 =$ ___

30. $8 * 2 =$ ___

31. $7 \times 9 =$ ___

32. $6 * 6 =$ ___

33. $1 * 4 =$ ___

34. $6 \cdot 8 =$ ___

35. $4 \times 5 =$ ___

36. $6 * 7 =$ ___

37. $80 / 10 =$ ___

38. $\frac{9}{3} =$ ___

39. $27 \div 9 =$ ___

40. $15 \div 5 =$ ___

41. $24 / 4 =$ ___

42. $8\overline{)72}$

43. $32 \div 4 =$ ___

44. $7\overline{)35}$

45. $\frac{12}{6} =$ ___

46. $0 / 8 =$ ___

47. $70 \div 7 =$ ___

48. $\frac{21}{3} =$ ___

49. $7\overline{)56}$

50. $36 / 6 =$ ___

51. $\frac{24}{8} =$ ___

52. $16 / 2 =$ ___

53. $4\overline{)40}$

54. $4 \div 1 =$ ___

55. $35 \div 5 =$ ___

56. $32 / 4 =$ ___

57. $2\overline{)8}$

58. $54 \div 9 =$ ___

59. $27 / 3 =$ ___

60. $24 \div 6 =$ ___

61. $21 / 7 =$ ___

62. $42 \div 6 =$ ___

63. $8\overline{)40}$

64. $15 / 3 =$ ___

65. $36 \div 9 =$ ___

66. $49 / 7 =$ ___

67. $12 \div 2 =$ ___

68. $48 / 6 =$ ___

69. $\frac{16}{4} =$ ___

70. $63 / 7 =$ ___

71. $8\overline{)56}$

72. $40 \div 5 =$ ___

Class Activity

► Read Tables

Johanna collected information about the type, weight, and lifespan of several dog breeds. Information like this is **data**. Johanna organized the data into a **table**. A table uses **rows** and **columns** to display information.

Dog Breed Information			
Breed	**Type of Dog**	**Average Weight (pounds)**	**Average Lifespan (years)**
Pug	Toy	16	13
Yorkshire terrier	Toy	5	13
Dachshund	Hound	24	11
Bloodhound	Hound	95	11
Boxer	Working	65	9
Great Dane	Working	115	7
Labrador retriever	Sporting	65	11
Cocker spaniel	Sporting	26	13
Dalmatian	Nonsporting	55	11
Boston terrier	Nonsporting	17	14
Australian cattle dog	Herding	44	11
German shepherd	Herding	80	12
Jack Russell terrier	Terrier	12	14
Bull terrier	Terrier	55	12

1. What is the average weight of a dachshund?

   _____

2. Which breed in the table has the shortest lifespan?

   _____

3. Which two dogs are sporting dogs?

   _____

   _____

4. What is the difference in average weight between a Great Dane and a Jack Russell terrier?

   _____

5. **Math Journal** Make up your own question about the information in the table. Answer your question.

Solve Word Problems With Tables

Class Activity

▶ Make a Table

6. Make a table with information about members of your group. One column should show information that is numbers. The other should show information that is words.

Student's Name		

7. Make up at least three questions about your table.

_____

_____

_____

_____

_____

_____

_____

_____

_____

_____

_____

_____

_____

_____

Going Further

Vocabulary

function
rule

▶ Discuss Function Rules

A **function** is a mathematical rule. A **rule** can be made up of words, numbers, or words and numbers. "A ladybug has 6 legs" is an example of a rule.

A table can be used to show the relationship between the number of ladybugs and the number of legs.

ladybugs	1	2	3	4	5	6
legs	6	12	18	24	30	36

1. Explain how you could use the table to predict the number of legs 10 ladybugs would have.

_____

_____

2. How many legs do 10 ladybugs have altogether?

_____

For each rule, complete the table. Answer each question.

3. One nickel is the same amount of money as 5 pennies.

nickels	1	2	3	4	5	6	7
pennies	5	10	15	20			

4. How many pennies are equal to the value of 20 nickels? Explain how you know.

_____

5. Each movie ticket costs $8.

tickets	1	2	3	4	5	6	7
cost	$8	$16	$24	$32			

6. What would be the total cost of tickets for a group of 15 people? Explain how you know.

_____

Class Activity

Vocabulary

combinations

► **Complete and Interpret a Table**

A restaurant makes veggie pizzas with 2 types of crust (thick or thin) and 5 toppings (pineapple, mushrooms, onions, green peppers, or black olives). You can use a table to show all the possible one-topping pizzas.

1. Complete the table.

	Pineapple	Mushrooms	Onions	Green Peppers	Black Olives
Thick	pineapple on thick crust				
Thin					

Look at the rows in the table.

2. How many one-topping pizzas have thick crust? _____

3. How many one-topping pizzas have thin crust? _____

4. What addition equation could you write to show the total number of one-topping pizzas? _____

5. What multiplication equation could you write? _____

Now look at the columns in the table.

6. For each topping, how many different pizzas are possible? _____

7. What addition equation could you write to show the total number of one-topping pizzas? _____

8. What multiplication equation could you write? _____

9. **Math Connection** Describe how finding the total number of combinations is like finding the total for an array.

_____

▶ Create and Use Tables

On a separate sheet of paper, make a table to show all the possible combinations. Then write a multiplication equation to show the total number of combinations.

10. Rashawn has blue, green, red, and white T-shirts. He has black, blue, and tan pants. How many different outfits can he make?

11. A gift-wrapping service has 4 kinds of wrapping paper — plain, flowers, polka dots, and stripes — and 5 colors of ribbon — green, red, blue, yellow, and pink. How many different combinations of paper and ribbon are there?

▶ Use Any Method

Show your work.

Solve.

12. Mr. Estrada has blue, white, gray, and pink dress shirts. He has a plain tie and a striped tie. How many different shirt-and-tie combinations can he make?

13. There are 8 girls and 7 boys in the school play. A boy and a girl will talk about the play at the school assembly. How many combinations of 1 boy and 1 girl are possible?

14. Joe's restaurant combines any pasta with any sauce to offer 18 combinations in all. If there are 3 types of pasta, how many types of sauce are there?

$7\overline{)5}$ $5\overline{)4}$ $2\overline{)4}$ $4\overline{)8}$ $7\overline{)4}$ $6\overline{)4}$

$6\overline{)2}$ $10\overline{)8}$ $6\overline{)5}$ $1\overline{)7}$ $3\overline{)7}$ $1\overline{)8}$

$9\overline{)8}$ $8\overline{)7}$ $9\overline{)6}$ $6\overline{)9}$ $10\overline{)6}$ $4\overline{)7}$

$8\overline{)1}$ $4\overline{)6}$ $2\overline{)6}$ $8\overline{)5}$ $1\overline{)6}$ $7\overline{)3}$

$5\overline{)6}$ $7\overline{)7}$ $8\overline{)9}$ $5\overline{)7}$ $8\overline{)8}$ $5\overline{)8}$

$2\overline{)8}$ $9\overline{)7}$ $7\overline{)2}$ $3\overline{)8}$ $7\overline{)0}$ $10\overline{)7}$

$6\overline{)1}$ $6\overline{)10}$ $3\overline{)6}$ $8\overline{)2}$ $10\overline{)4}$ $6\overline{)3}$

$8\overline{)6}$ $9\overline{)4}$ $8\overline{)3}$ $6\overline{)6}$ $2\overline{)7}$ $8\overline{)4}$

$7\overline{)9}$ $6\overline{)8}$ $3\overline{)4}$ $7\overline{)6}$ $7\overline{)8}$ $7\overline{)10}$

$4\overline{)4}$ $7\overline{)1}$ $8\overline{)0}$ $8\overline{)10}$ $6\overline{)0}$ $6\overline{)7}$

8)80	8)24	7)7	8)16	2)14	7)49
5)30	6)42	4)16	7)42	10)80	8)48
7)21	10)70	6)24	6)0	7)63	3)21
3)18	5)40	8)56	6)48	6)18	9)72
8)32	9)54	2)12	10)60	1)6	4)28
6)12	4)32	9)63	7)14	5)35	8)8
4)24	7)56	6)60	1)7	8)40	6)54
7)70	2)8	3)24	3)12	6)30	10)40
2)16	6)36	6)6	9)36	8)72	8)0
7)35	1)8	8)64	7)0	5)20	7)28

Class Write-On Sheet 2B

$7 \overline{)35}$ = 5 $5 \overline{)20}$ = 4 $2 \overline{)8}$ = 4 $4 \overline{)32}$ = 8 $7 \overline{)28}$ = 4 $6 \overline{)24}$ = 4

$6 \overline{)12}$ = 2 $10 \overline{)80}$ = 8 $6 \overline{)30}$ = 5 $1 \overline{)7}$ = 7 $3 \overline{)21}$ = 7 $1 \overline{)8}$ = 8

$9 \overline{)72}$ = 8 $8 \overline{)56}$ = 7 $9 \overline{)54}$ = 6 $6 \overline{)54}$ = 9 $10 \overline{)60}$ = 6 $4 \overline{)28}$ = 7

$8 \overline{)8}$ = 1 $4 \overline{)24}$ = 6 $2 \overline{)12}$ = 6 $8 \overline{)40}$ = 5 $1 \overline{)6}$ = 6 $7 \overline{)21}$ = 3

$5 \overline{)30}$ = 6 $7 \overline{)49}$ = 7 $8 \overline{)72}$ = 9 $5 \overline{)35}$ = 7 $8 \overline{)64}$ = 8 $5 \overline{)40}$ = 8

$2 \overline{)16}$ = 8 $9 \overline{)63}$ = 7 $7 \overline{)14}$ = 2 $3 \overline{)24}$ = 8 $7 \overline{)0}$ = 0 $10 \overline{)70}$ = 7

$6 \overline{)6}$ = 1 $6 \overline{)60}$ = 10 $3 \overline{)18}$ = 6 $8 \overline{)16}$ = 2 $10 \overline{)40}$ = 4 $6 \overline{)18}$ = 3

$8 \overline{)48}$ = 6 $9 \overline{)36}$ = 4 $8 \overline{)24}$ = 3 $6 \overline{)36}$ = 6 $2 \overline{)14}$ = 7 $8 \overline{)32}$ = 4

$7 \overline{)63}$ = 9 $6 \overline{)48}$ = 8 $3 \overline{)12}$ = 4 $7 \overline{)42}$ = 6 $7 \overline{)56}$ = 8 $7 \overline{)70}$ = 10

$4 \overline{)16}$ = 4 $7 \overline{)7}$ = 1 $8 \overline{)0}$ = 0 $8 \overline{)80}$ = 10 $6 \overline{)0}$ = 0 $6 \overline{)42}$ = 7

$\overset{10}{8\overline{)80}}$	$\overset{3}{8\overline{)24}}$	$\overset{1}{7\overline{)7}}$	$\overset{2}{8\overline{)16}}$	$\overset{7}{2\overline{)14}}$	$\overset{7}{7\overline{)49}}$
$\overset{6}{5\overline{)30}}$	$\overset{7}{6\overline{)42}}$	$\overset{4}{4\overline{)16}}$	$\overset{6}{7\overline{)42}}$	$\overset{8}{10\overline{)80}}$	$\overset{6}{8\overline{)48}}$
$\overset{3}{7\overline{)21}}$	$\overset{7}{10\overline{)70}}$	$\overset{4}{6\overline{)24}}$	$\overset{0}{6\overline{)0}}$	$\overset{9}{7\overline{)63}}$	$\overset{7}{3\overline{)21}}$
$\overset{6}{3\overline{)18}}$	$\overset{8}{5\overline{)40}}$	$\overset{7}{8\overline{)56}}$	$\overset{8}{6\overline{)48}}$	$\overset{3}{6\overline{)18}}$	$\overset{8}{9\overline{)72}}$
$\overset{4}{8\overline{)32}}$	$\overset{6}{9\overline{)54}}$	$\overset{6}{2\overline{)12}}$	$\overset{6}{10\overline{)60}}$	$\overset{6}{1\overline{)6}}$	$\overset{7}{4\overline{)28}}$
$\overset{2}{6\overline{)12}}$	$\overset{8}{4\overline{)32}}$	$\overset{7}{9\overline{)63}}$	$\overset{2}{7\overline{)14}}$	$\overset{7}{5\overline{)35}}$	$\overset{1}{8\overline{)8}}$
$\overset{6}{4\overline{)24}}$	$\overset{8}{7\overline{)56}}$	$\overset{10}{6\overline{)60}}$	$\overset{7}{1\overline{)7}}$	$\overset{5}{8\overline{)40}}$	$\overset{9}{6\overline{)54}}$
$\overset{10}{7\overline{)70}}$	$\overset{4}{2\overline{)8}}$	$\overset{8}{3\overline{)24}}$	$\overset{4}{3\overline{)12}}$	$\overset{5}{6\overline{)30}}$	$\overset{4}{10\overline{)40}}$
$\overset{8}{2\overline{)16}}$	$\overset{6}{6\overline{)36}}$	$\overset{1}{6\overline{)6}}$	$\overset{4}{9\overline{)36}}$	$\overset{9}{8\overline{)72}}$	$\overset{0}{8\overline{)0}}$
$\overset{5}{7\overline{)35}}$	$\overset{8}{1\overline{)8}}$	$\overset{8}{8\overline{)64}}$	$\overset{0}{7\overline{)0}}$	$\overset{4}{5\overline{)20}}$	$\overset{4}{7\overline{)28}}$

Class Check Sheet 2B

Class Activity

▶ Factor Triangles and Fast Arrays

Fill in the unknown number in each Factor Triangle.

1.
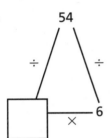

2.
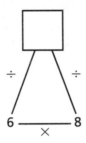

3.
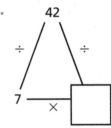

4.
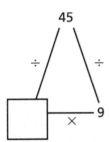

5.
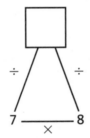

6.
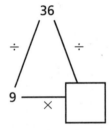

Fill in the unknown number in each Fast Array.

7.   7
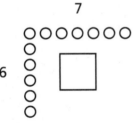

8.   8
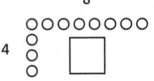

9.
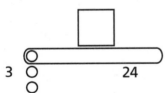

10.
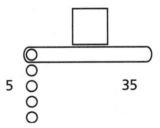

11. **On the Back** Draw two Factor Triangles and two Fast Arrays. Then write a multiplication and a division equation for each.

Factor Triangle	Factor Triangle
_____ _____	_____ _____
Fast Array	**Fast Array**
_____ _____	_____ _____

▶ **Discuss Comparison Problems**

To prepare for a family gathering, Sara and Ryan made soup. Sara made 2 quarts. Ryan made 6 quarts.

You can **compare** amounts using multiplication and division.

Let *r* equal the number of quarts Ryan made.
Let *s* equal the number of quarts Sara made.

Ryan made 3 times as many quarts as Sara.

$$r = 3 \cdot s$$

Sara made one-third as many quarts as Ryan.

$$s = \frac{1}{3} \cdot r \text{ or } s = r \div 3$$

| Ryan (r) | 2 | 2 | 2 | 6 |
| Sarah (s) | 2 | 2 | 2 | |

Solve.

Natasha made 12 quarts of soup. Manuel made 3 quarts.

1. Draw **comparison bars** to show the amount of soup each person made.

2. _____ made 4 times as many quarts as _____.

3. Write a multiplication equation that compares the amounts. _____

4. _____ made $\frac{1}{4}$ as many quarts as _____.

5. Write a division equation that compares the amounts. _____

6. Multiplication is the putting together of equal groups. How can this idea be used to explain why a *times as many* comparing situation is multiplication?

_____

_____

▶ Share Solutions

Solve.

In the gym, 8 girls are standing in one line and 4 boys are standing in another line.

7. Draw comparison bars to compare the number of people in each line.

8. Write a multiplication equation that compares the number of girls (*g*) to the number of boys (*b*).

   _____

9. Write a division equation that compares the number of boys (*b*) to the number of girls (*g*).

   _____

10. A collection of coins contains 20 pennies and 4 nickels.

    Write a multiplication equation and a division equation that compares the number of pennies (*p*) and the number of nickels (*n*).

    _____   _____

11. A fourth grade class is made up of 12 boys and 24 girls. How many times as many girls as boys are in the class?

    _____

12. Jessica ran 100 meters. This distance was 5 times as many meters as Lisa ran. What distance did Lisa run?

    _____

13. Fred has 24 football cards. Scott has $\frac{1}{6}$ as many football cards as Fred. How many football cards does Scott have?

Multiplication Comparisons

Class Activity

Name _____ Date _____

Vocabulary

pictograph

▶ Use a Pictograph

A **pictograph** can be used to compare amounts. The pictograph
shows how many books 5 students checked out of the library for one month.

Books Checked Out of Library	
Student	
Najee	📖 📖
Tariq	📖 📖 📖 📖 📖 📖
Celine	📖 📖 📖 📖 📖 📖 📖 📖
Jamarcus	📖 📖 📖
Brooke	📖 📖 📖 📖

📖 = 5 books

Use the pictograph to solve.

1. Write a multiplication equation that compares the
   number of books Tariq checked out (*t*) to the number
   of books Jamarcus checked out (*j*).

   _____

2. Write a division equation that compares the number of
   books Najee checked out (*n*) to the number of books
   Celine checked out (*c*).

   _____

3. Celine checked out twice as many books as which student?

   _____

4. Which student checked out $\frac{1}{4}$ as many books as Celine?

   _____

5. The number of books Dawson checked out is not shown.
   If Jamarcus took three times as many books as Dawson,
   how many books did Dawson check out?

   _____

6. **On the Back** Write two sentences about the graph that
   contain the words *times as many*.

Mixed Comparison Problems

Name _____ **Date** _____

Class Activity

► Use a Vertical Bar Graph

The **vertical bar graph** below shows the number of home runs hit by five members of a baseball team.

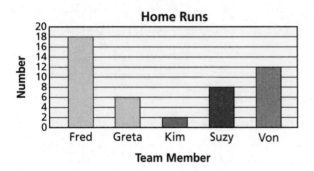

7. Write a multiplication equation that compares the number of home runs Suzy hit (*s*) to the number of home runs Kim hit (*k*).

_____

8. Write a division equation that compares the number of home runs Greta hit (*g*) to the number of runs Fred hit (*f*).

_____

9. How many times as many home runs did Von hit as Greta?

_____

10. Which player hit $\frac{1}{6}$ as many home runs as Von?

_____

11. This year, Fred hit twice as many home runs as he hit last year. How many home runs did Fred hit last year?

_____

12. Write a sentence about the graph that contains the words *times as many*.

_____

_____

Name _____ **Date** _____

► Conduct a Survey

Choose a survey topic from the box or make up one of your own. Conduct your survey and record your results in the tally chart.

Which _____ do you like best?	
Answer Choices	Tally

Use the tally chart to draw a horizontal bar graph.

_____

Mixed Comparison Problems

Class Activity

▶ **Discuss Horizontal Bar Graphs**

Discuss the **horizontal bar graph** with your class.

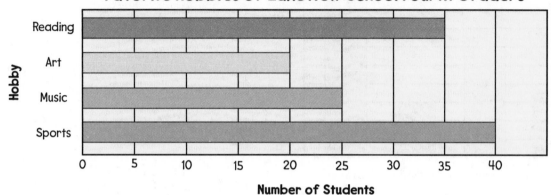

Favorite Hobbies of Lakeview School Fourth Graders

Use the bar graph to answer the questions below.

1. How many fourth grade students said reading was their favorite hobby? _____

2. Which hobby is most popular? _____ How many students chose it? _____

3. What hobby is half as popular as sports? _____

4. How many more students picked reading than art? _____

5. Altogether, how many students picked art or music? _____

6. Write your own question about the graph. Answer your question.

_____

_____

_____

Class Activity

Vocabulary
vertical bar graph

▶ Discuss Vertical Bar Graphs

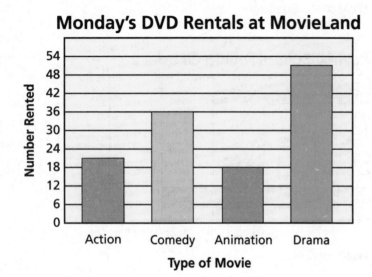

Monday's DVD Rentals at MovieLand

Use the vertical bar graph to answer the questions below.

7. How many DVDs rented on Monday were dramas? _____

8. What was the least popular type of movie? _____

9. How many fewer animation movies were rented than comedy movies? _____

10. Is the total number of action and animation DVDs rented more or less than the number of drama DVDs rented? _____ How much more or less? _____

11. What is the total number rented on Monday? _____

12. Write and answer a question about the graph.

_____

_____

_____

Class Activity

▶ Create a Bar Graph

Use the information in the table to create a bar graph.

Points Scored in Last Game	
Player	**Points**
Corey	6
Ming	18
Tamara	11
Hannah	10
Luisa	20

Things to Think About
- Will your bar graph be vertical or horizontal?
- Which axis will have the scale?
- What should the greatest scale value be? What should be the interval between scale values?
- What will the bars represent? How many bars will you have?
- How should you label the axes?
- What should the title be?

Going Further

Vocabulary	
tally chart	range
frequency table	mode
line plot	median

▶ Charts, Tables, and Line Plots

The heights of some students in a fourth grade class may be shown in different ways.

A **tally chart** records and organizes data.

A **frequency table** lists how many times events occur.

A **line plot** is a diagram that shows the frequency of data on a number line.

Tally Chart

Height	Tally
47	/
48	//
49	////
50	///
51	/
52	
53	//

Frequency Table

Height	Frequency
47	1
48	2
49	4
50	3
51	1
52	0
53	2
Total	13

Line Plot

```
                    X
                  X   X
              X   X   X           X
          X   X   X   X   X       X
          ┬───┬───┬───┬───┬───┬───┬
          47  48  49  50  51  52  53
```
Heights of Students

Three different measures can be used to describe the data.

The **range** is the difference between the greatest value and least value in a set.	The **mode** is the value that appears most frequently in a set of data values.	The **median** is the middle number in a set of ordered data values.
The range for this data is **6** because 53 − 47 = 6.	The mode for this data is **49** because that value occurs most.	The median for this data is **49** because out of 13 values the middle value is 49. 47 48 48 49 49 49 **49** 50 50 50 51 53 53

On a separate sheet of paper, make a tally chart, frequency table, and line plot for the data at the right.

Number of hours some students did homework last week:

4, 7, 2, 3, 8, 1, 0, 3, 5, 3, 2, 2, 1, 5, 2

Going Further

▶ Guess and Check

Use the Guess and Check strategy if there is no clear way to solve a problem. Use the facts given in the problem to make a reasonable guess. Then check your guess. Keep guessing until your check shows that you guessed the right answer. You can use a table to organize your guesses and checks.

Tim bought three times as many books as Sara. Together, they bought 24 books. How many books did they each buy?

Step 1 Guess a number of books for Sara.

Step 2 Multiply that guess by 3 to get Tim's number of books.

Step 3 Add the two guesses to check if they total 24 books.

Answer: Sara bought 6 books and Tim bought 18 books.

Guess		Check	
Sara	Tim	Total	Is it 24?
8	8 × 3 = 24	8 + 24 = 32	No
7	7 × 3 = 21	7 + 21 = 28	No
6	6 × 3 = 18	6 + 18 = 24	Yes!

Use the Guess and Check strategy to solve each problem.

1. Antwan is twice as old as Maria. The sum of their ages is 18 years. How old is Antwan? How old is Maria?

2. A rectangular patio has a perimeter of 36 yards. It is twice as long as it is wide. What is the length and width of the patio?

3. Wendy made 20 apple and cherry pies. She made three times as many apple pies as cherry pies. How many of each kind of pie did she make?

4. There are 45 students in the math club. There are four times as many girls as boys in the club. How many boys are in the club? How many girls?

5. **On the Back** Write a problem that can be solved with the Guess and Check strategy.

Name _____ **Date** _____

_____

_____

_____

_____

_____

_____

_____

_____

_____

_____

_____

_____

_____

_____

_____

_____

_____

_____

_____

Fluency Day

Class Activity

| Name | Date |

▶ Order of Operations

Solve.

1. $6 \times 8 - 4 =$ _____

2. $6 \times (8 - 4) =$ _____

3. $5 + 2 \times 9 =$ _____

4. $(6 \times 5) + (2 \times 9) =$ _____

5. $(3 + 2) \times 6 =$ _____

6. $4 \times 6 + 8 =$ _____

7. $(4 + 3) \times (2 + 2) =$ _____

8. $7 \times (10 - 9) =$ _____

▶ Discuss the Steps of the Problem

Solve.

9. Darrin made 8 batches of chocolate chip cookies for his friends. Each batch had 6 cookies. He overcooked the first batch and threw those cookies away. How many cookies did Darrin serve to his friends? _____

10. Mike's Bike Shop replaced all the tires on 6 bicycles on Tuesday. The shop replaced the tires on 5 tricycles on Wednesday. How many total tires did Mike's Bike Shop replace on Tuesday and Wednesday? _____

11. Marlon has $20 to spend at the movie theater. He wants to buy 2 movie tickets for $4.00 each and 3 small popcorn bags for $2.00 each. Will Marlon have enough money to spend at the theater? _____

Show your work.

Class Activity

► **Solve Multi-Step Word Problems**

Solve.

12. Eli reads 6 pages in a book each night. Shelby reads 7 pages each night. How many pages all together will Eli and Shelby read in one week?

_____

13. Felicia has 32 marbles. Sabrena had half as many marbles as Felicia, and then she bought 4 more. How many marbles does Sabrena have?

_____

14. Min Soo ordered 5 different cakes for a party. Each cake was cut into 8 slices. Three cakes were carrot cake, and the rest were chocolate cake. How many slices of cake did Min Soo have in all?

_____

15. Team A and Team B have 17 players each. Team A has 6 girls. Team B has twice as many girls as Team A. How many girls play on both teams? How many boys play on both teams?

_____

16. Jasmine and Mori each received the same number of party favor bags at a friend's party. The bags contained 8 favors each. If Jasmine and Mori had 48 party favors total, how many party favor bags did they each receive?

_____

17. Ernesto made some candy dishes in art class for his mother and brother. Each dish can hold 9 pieces of candy. Ernesto's brother fit 18 pieces of candy into his dishes. His mother fit 36 pieces of candy into hers. How many candy dishes did Ernesto make?

_____

18. **Write Your Own** Write a problem that must be solved using more than one step.

_____

_____

_____

▶ Checkup D: 2s, 5s, 9s, 3s, 4s, 6s, 7s, 8s, 1s, 0s

1. $5 * 3 =$ ___

2. $9 / 3 =$ ___

3. $4\overline{)28}$

4. $6 \cdot 6 =$ ___

5. $\frac{81}{9} =$ ___

6. $42 \div 6 =$ ___

7. $7 \times 9 =$ ___

8. $18 / 9 =$ ___

9. $6 * 7 =$ ___

10. $2 \cdot 8 =$ ___

11. $8\overline{)32}$

12. $\frac{6}{3} =$ ___

13. $24 \div 3 =$ ___

14. $4 \times 7 =$ ___

15. $2 * 9 =$ ___

16. $12 / 3 =$ ___

17. $9\overline{)45}$

18. $5 \cdot 6 =$ ___

19. $1 \times 8 =$ ___

20. $7 * 4 =$ ___

21. $16 \div 8 =$ ___

22. $56 / 7 =$ ___

23. $4\overline{)32}$

24. $0 \cdot 3 =$ ___

25. $9 \times 8 =$ ___

26. $\frac{12}{4} =$ ___

27. $2 * 7 =$ ___

28. $8 \cdot 6 =$ ___

29. $36 \div 9 =$ ___

30. $3 \times 8 =$ ___

31. $54 / 9 =$ ___

32. $9 * 7 =$ ___

33. $8 \cdot 3 =$ ___

34. $4\overline{)36}$

35. $\frac{0}{7} =$ ___

36. $48 \div 8 =$ ___

37. $3 \times 3 =$ ___

38. $9 * 6 =$ ___

39. $63 / 7 =$ ___

40. $6\overline{)18}$

41. $8 \cdot 4 =$ ___

42. $6 \times 3 =$ ___

43. $\frac{63}{9} =$ ___

44. $2 * 6 =$ ___

45. $8 \div 4 =$ ___

46. $3 \cdot 4 =$ ___

47. $30 / 6 =$ ___

48. $7 \times 7 =$ ___

49. $7\overline{)42}$

50. $4 * 6 =$ ___

51. $\frac{36}{6} =$ ___

52. $6 \cdot 8 =$ ___

53. $27 \div 3 =$ ___

54. $4 \times 3 =$ ___

55. $24 / 4 =$ ___

56. $7\overline{)21}$

57. $2 * 3 =$ ___

58. $\frac{40}{8} =$ ___

59. $15 \div 3 =$ ___

60. $27 / 9 =$ ___

61. $8\overline{)24}$

62. $5 \cdot 9 =$ ___

63. $6 \times 4 =$ ___

64. $\frac{18}{3} =$ ___

65. $64 \div 8 =$ ___

66. $24 / 6 =$ ___

67. $3 * 6 =$ ___

68. $6\overline{)6}$

69. $\frac{20}{4} =$ ___

70. $3 * 7 =$ ___

71. $12 \div 6 =$ ___

72. $9 \times 9 =$ ___

▶ **Factor Fireworks**

A **factor pair** for a number is two whole numbers whose product is that number. For example, 2 and 5 is a factor pair for 10.

A number greater than 1 that has 1 and itself as its only factor pair is a **prime number**. Some prime numbers are 2, 5, 11, and 23.

A number greater than 1 that has more than one factor pair is a **composite number**. Some composite numbers are 4, 12, 25, and 100.

The number 1 is neither prime nor composite.

Factor Fireworks show how a whole number can be broken down into a product of prime numbers. At the right are two Factor Fireworks for 12. This way of showing factors is also called a **Factor Tree**.

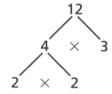 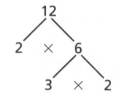

It doesn't matter how large a whole number is; you can always break it down into a product of prime numbers. At the right is a Factor Fireworks for 21,000.

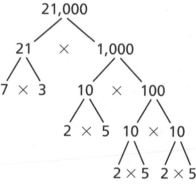

No matter what factor pair you start with, you will always get the same prime numbers at the ends of the branches. Below are three Factor Fireworks for 36. What 4 factors are at the bottom of each of these Factor Fireworks?

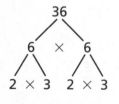 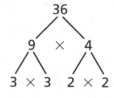 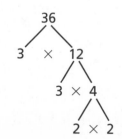

Factors and Prime Numbers

▶ Use Prime Factors to Divide

1. Make Factor Fireworks for the number 56.

2. Write an equation that shows 56 as a product of prime numbers.

_____

3. Use your equation to help you find 56 ÷ 14.

_____

4. Make Factor Fireworks for the number 72.

5. Write an equation that shows 72 as a product of prime factors.

_____

6. Use your equation to help you find 72 ÷ 12.

_____

Darnell said, "If you make a Factor Fireworks for an even number, you always have at least one 2 at the ends of the branches. If you make one for an odd number, you don't get any 2s."

7. On the Back Experiment by making Factor Fireworks for a few even and odd numbers. Do you think Darnell is right? Explain.

Factors and Prime Numbers

Solve each word problem.

Show your work.

1. Juan and Tina are making cracker snacks. They have 4 kinds of spreads and 7 food toppings for the spreads. They always use one spread and one food topping on each cracker snack. How many different kinds of cracker snacks can they make in all?

   _____

2. There are 36 desks in Jan's classroom. If there are 9 rows of desks, how many desks are in each row?

   _____

3. James has 35 model cars. His bookcase has 5 shelves. If he puts the same number of cars on each shelf, how many cars does each shelf have?

   _____

4. A car company has 15 combinations of outside and inside colors. For the inside they have black, tan, or gray. How many different outside colors do they have?

   _____

The bar graph shows the number of students in each grade at Central Elementary School.

5. Which grade has $\frac{1}{2}$ as many students as fourth grade?

   _____

6. Which grade has three times as many students as first grade?

   _____

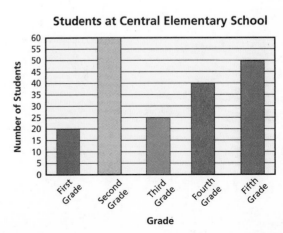

Students at Central Elementary School

U1–Test

Name _____   **Date** _____

Write eight equations for the Fast Array.

7.   9

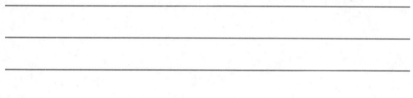

4   36

_____   _____

_____   _____

_____   _____

_____   _____

Fill in the blanks to show how the Associative Property of Multiplication works.

8. $(2 \times 3) \times 4 =$ _____ $\times$ (_____ $\times$ _____)

9. Describe 2 patterns in the 9s count-bys.

_____

_____

Solve the word problem.

10. **Extended Response** Sam bought 7 hats for $6 each. He paid with a $50 bill. How much change did he receive? Explain how you found your answer.

_____

_____

_____

_____

Name _____   Date _____

Vocabulary

plane
congruent

▶ Explore Congruence

Sherrie used one side of a small box to trace two figures.

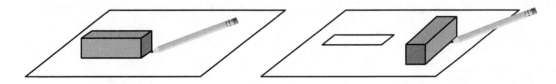

1. Which picture shows her paper? How do you know?

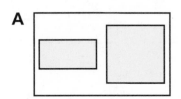 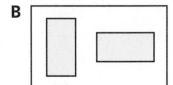 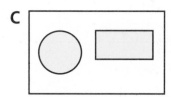

_____   _____   _____

_____   _____   _____

Two-dimensional (2-D) figures are called **plane** figures.
They are **congruent** when they are exactly the same size
and shape.

2. Do the figures on Sherrie's paper look congruent?
Why or why not?

_____

_____

3. Which two figures look congruent? Explain how you know.

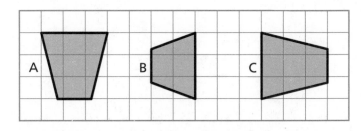

_____

_____

▶ Identify Congruent Figures

Do all the figures in each group look congruent?
Explain your thinking.

4.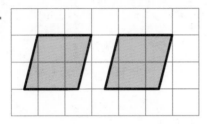

_____

5.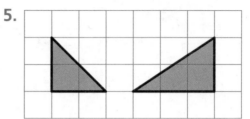

_____

6.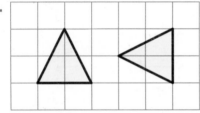

_____

7.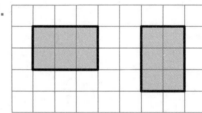

_____

8.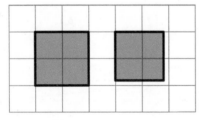

_____

9.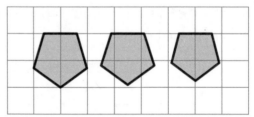

_____

10.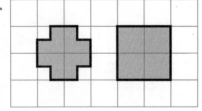

_____

11.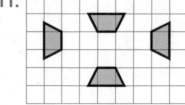

_____

Vocabulary

line symmetry
line of symmetry

►**Identify Lines of Symmetry**

A plane figure has **line symmetry** if you can fold it to make two parts that are mirror images. The fold is called a **line of symmetry**.

Which figures have line symmetry?

12.
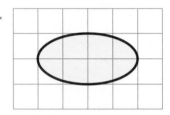

13.
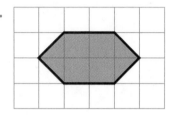

14.
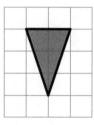

_____

_____

_____

15.
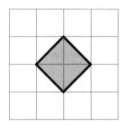

16.
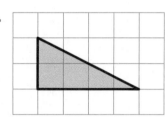

17.
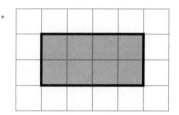

_____

_____

_____

18. Which figures have more than one line of symmetry? _____

Draw the other half of each figure to make a whole figure with line symmetry.

19.
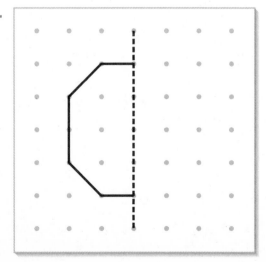

20.
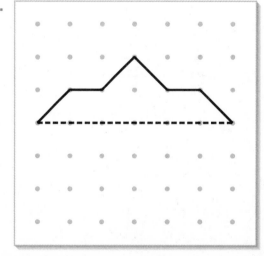

Going Further

▶ Explore Reflections

Draw a **reflection** of each figure on the opposite side
of the dotted line.

1.
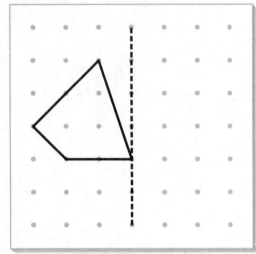

2.
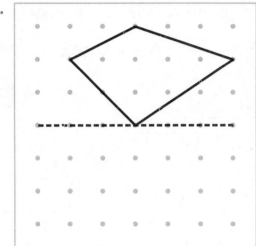

3.
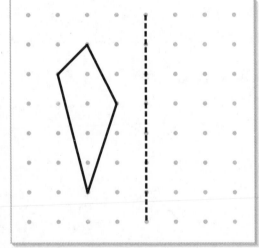

4.
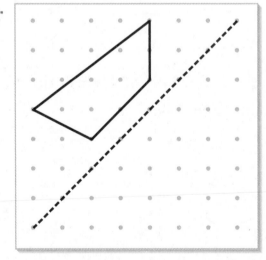

Congruence and Symmetry

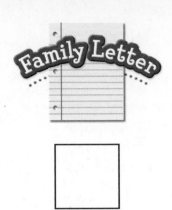

Dear Family,

Your child will be learning about geometry throughout the school year. This first unit is about a group of geometric figures called quadrilaterals, which get their name because they have four (*quad-*) sides (*-lateral*). Four different kinds of quadrilaterals are shown here.

In this unit, your child will also learn the difference between perimeter and area. Area drawings help children to understand multi-digit multiplication.

For example:

Square
4 equal sides
opposite sides parallel
right angles

$$4 \times 26 = 104$$

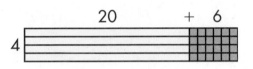

Rectangle
2 pairs of parallel sides
right angles

$$80 + 24 = 104$$

We urge you to encourage regular home practice of the basic multiplications and divisions. We will return to more of them in about a week. Later in the year, we will be learning about both multi-digit multiplication and multi-digit division.

Rhombus
4 equal sides
opposite sides parallel

If you have any questions or comments, please call or write to me.

Sincerely,
Your child's teacher

Parallelogram
2 pairs of parallel sides

Cuadrado
4 lados iguales
lados opuestos paralelos
ángulos rectos

Rectángulo
2 pares de lados paralelos
ángulos rectos

Rombo
4 lados iguales
lados opuestos paralelos

Paralelogramo
2 pares de lados paralelos

Estimada familia:

Durante el año escolar, su niño aprenderá geometría. La primera unidad trata de un grupo de figuras geométricas llamadas cuadriláteros, las cuales reciben este nombre porque tienen cuatro (*cuad-*) lados (*latero*). Aquí se muestran cuatro tipos diferentes de cuadriláteros.

En esta unidad, su niño también aprenderá la diferencia entre perímetro y área. Los dibujos de áreas ayudarán a comprender la multiplicación con números de más de un dígito.

Por ejemplo:

$$4 \times 26 = 104$$

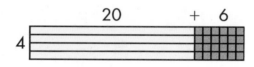

$$80 + 24 = 104$$

Recomendamos que anime a su niño a práticar las multiplicaciones y divisiones básicas en casa. En una semana veremos más de éstas. Más adelante en el año aprenderemos a multiplicar y a dividir con números de más de un dígito.

Si tiene alguna pregunta o comentario, por favor comuníquese conmigo.

Atentamente,
El maestro de su niño

Congruence and Symmetry

► **Sort and Name Figures**

Examine these figures.

A    B    C   D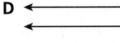

E 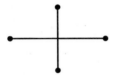   F   G   H

I    J   K   L

M 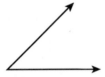   N    O   P

1. How are some of the figures alike?

_____

_____

_____

2. How do some of the figures differ from one another?

_____

_____

_____

Vocabulary

perpendicular
right angle
parallel

▶ Sort and Name Figures (continued)

Use the figures on the previous page.

3. A **line** is straight and continues forever in both directions. You can say that a figure is a line or you can draw arrowheads on its ends to say that it extends forever. Which figures show lines?

_____

line

4. A **line segment** has a fixed length. If a figure is a line segment, it cannot be made longer. You can add points at the ends of the line segment to show that it cannot be made longer. Which figures show line segments?

_____

line segment

5. A **ray** begins at a point and can go on forever, but in only one direction. Which figures show rays?

_____

ray

6. When lines, line segments, or rays meet at a point, they form one or more **angles**. Which figures show angles?

_____

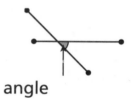

angle

7. When two lines, line segments, or rays cross and form four congruent angles, the lines are **perpendicular** and the angles made are **right angles**. Which figures look perpendicular?

_____

perpendicular line segments

8. When two lines are the same distance apart at every point they are called **parallel**. Which figures look as if the lines, rays, or line segments are parallel?

_____

parallel lines

Name _____ **Date** _____

Class Activity

Vocabulary
vertex
angle

▶ **Label Lines, Line Segments, Rays, and Angles**

You can name figures by labeling them with letters.

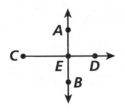

9. The letters *AB* name the line in this figure.
   Which letters name the ray in the figure? _____

10. A **vertex** is a point that is common to the two sides
    of an angle. One **angle** in this figure is ∠*AEC*. The
    middle letter of an angle's name indicates its vertex.

    Name three other angles in this figure. _____

**Name the line segments, vertex points, and angles
in each figure below.**

11.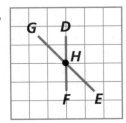

    Line segments: _____

    Vertex point: _____

    Angles: _____

12.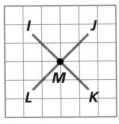

    Line segments: _____

    Vertex point: _____

    Angles: _____

13.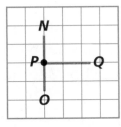

    Line segments: _____

    Vertex point: _____

    Angles: _____

14. Choose one of figures 11–13 and name the line segments
    and angles that look congruent.

    _____

► Label the Parts of Plane Figures

For each figure, name the sides that look parallel and those that look perpendicular. Not every example has both. Name at least one angle.

15.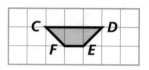

Parallel: _____

Perpendicular: _____

Angle: _____

16.

Parallel: _____

Perpendicular: _____

Angle: _____

17.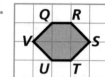

Parallel: _____

Perpendicular: _____

Angle: _____

18.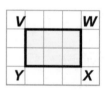

Parallel: _____

Perpendicular: _____

Angle: _____

19.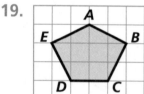

Parallel: _____

Perpendicular: _____

Angle: _____

20.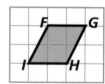

Parallel: _____

Perpendicular: _____

Angle: _____

► Draw Figures

21. Draw and label a figure with one pair of parallel line segments.

22. Draw and label a figure with one pair of perpendicular line segments.

Lines, Line Segments, and Rays

Class Activity

▶ Describe 4-Sided Figures

José has a new puppy named Daisy. He needs to build a four-sided dog pen in his yard for her. He wants us to help him plan a pen for Daisy.

1. Which of these figures could be Daisy's pen? _____

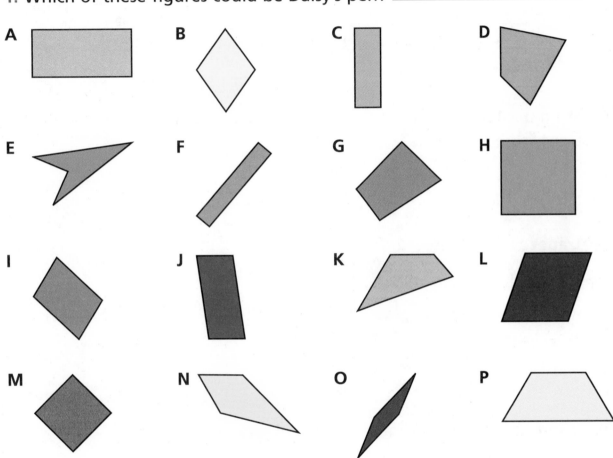

2. Which pens would Daisy probably like the most? Why?

_____

3. Look at the sides and angles of all the figures. Which figures can we group together because they are alike in some way?

_____

4. Which figures are alike in some way? Explain your answer.

_____

Name _____ **Date** _____

Class Activity

▶ **Name Some Quadrilaterals**

The prefix _quad-_ means "four." The suffix _-lateral_ means "sides."

5. Why are all of these figures called **quadrilaterals**?

_____

6. Talk with a partner about how each kind of quadrilateral is different from the others.

trapezoids

isosceles trapezoid

parallelogram

rhombus

rectangle

square

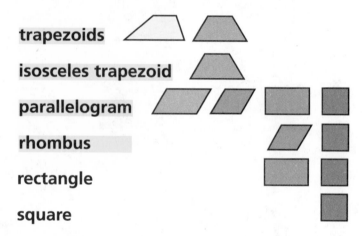

Complete exercises 7–10 on a separate sheet of paper.

7. Why are there several quadrilaterals in some of the rows in exercise 6?

Why is each sentence below true?

8. A rhombus is always a paralellogram, but a parallelogram isn't always a rhombus.

9. A rectangle is a parallelogram, but a parallelogram is not necessarily a rectangle.

10. A square is a rectangle, but a rectangle does not have to be a square.

Class Activity

▶ **Units of Perimeter**

The prefix *peri-* means "around." The suffix *-meter* means "measure." **Perimeter** is the measurement of the distance around the outside of a figure.

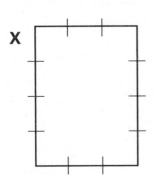

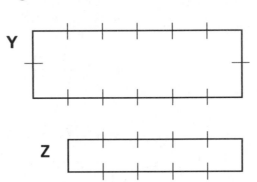

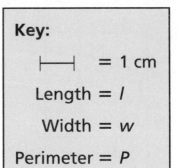

Key:

├──┤ = 1 cm

Length = *l*

Width = *w*

Perimeter = *P*

1. The measurement **unit** for these rectangles is 1 centimeter (1 cm). How can you find the total number of centimeters around the outside of each rectangle?

_____

_____

2. What is the perimeter of rectangle X? of rectangle Y? of rectangle Z?

_____

_____

3. What numeric method did you use to find each perimeter?

_____

_____

4. Look at the key: **length** is the distance across a rectangle and **width** is the distance up-and-down. Perimeter is the total distance around the outside. Use the letters *l, w,* and *P* to write a general equation for the perimeter of rectangles.

_____

Class Activity

Name

Date

▶ Units of Area

Area is the total number of **square units** inside a figure. Each square unit inside these rectangles is 1 cm long and 1 cm wide, so it is 1 square centimeter (1 sq cm).

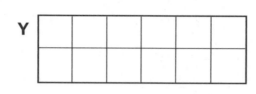

X

Y

Z

Key:

☐ = 1 sq cm

Length = l

Width = w

Area = A

5. How can you find the total number of square centimeters inside each rectangle?

_____

_____

6. What is the area of rectangle X? of rectangle Y? of rectangle Z?

_____

_____

7. Using l to stand for length, w to stand for width, and A to stand for area, what general equation can you write for finding the area of any rectangle?

_____

_____

8. Why does the same general equation work for all rectangles?

_____

_____

Class Activity

▶ Discuss Real-World Situations

Solve and discuss the word problems.

9. Taci's father made an array of square tiles on the bathroom floor before gluing them down. How many tiles across did his array have? How many tiles up-and-down? How many in all?

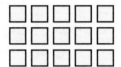

_____

_____

10. Taci wanted to know if the number of tiles in the array would be the same or different if her father took out the spaces between the tiles. What did her father tell her? Why?

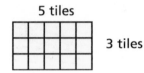

5 tiles

3 tiles

_____

_____

11. How does knowing about arrays help you to find the area of any rectangle?

_____

_____

12. The 15 tiles fit exactly in the bathroom without any spaces. If the measurement of one side of a single tile is 1 foot, what is the perimeter of the bathroom? What is its area?

_____

_____

13. If you know only the outside measurements for any rectangle, can you find its area? How? Why does this method work?

_____

_____

Class Activity

▶ Review Perimeter and Area

Perimeter and Area

Perimeter and area are measured with different kinds of units: units of distance or length for perimeter and square units for area.

Perimeter is the total distance around the outside of a figure.

This rectangle has 4 units along its length and 3 units along its width. To find the perimeter, you add the distances of all of the sides:

$$l + w + l + w = P$$

Area is the total number of square units inside a figure.

For rectangles, area can be seen as an array of squares. This rectangle is an array of 4 squares across (length) and 3 squares down (width). To find its area, you can multiply length times width:

$$l \times w = A$$

▶ Adapt the Equations

How can you change the equations for the area and perimeter of rectangles to apply to squares?

_____

_____

_____

_____

_____

_____

▶ Practice with Perimeter and Area

**For each pair of rectangles, tell which one shows units of
perimeter and find the perimeter. Tell which one shows
units of area and find the area. Use 1 inch as the unit of
length in all of your answers.**

14.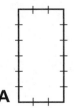

A   B

_____

_____

15.

A   B

_____

_____

16.

A   B

_____

_____

17.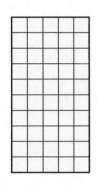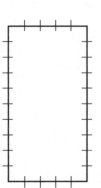

A   B

_____

_____

▶ Calculate Perimeter and Area

**On one figure, draw in the units of area and find the area.
On the other, draw in the units of perimeter and find
the perimeter.**

18.

9 mi

2 mi

2 mi

9 mi

P = _____

A = _____

19.

4 m

4 m

4 m

4 m

P = _____

A = _____

20.

6 cm

7 cm

7 cm

6 cm

P = _____

A = _____

21.

3 ft

5 ft

5 ft

3 ft

P = _____

A = _____

22. Challenge For one of the rectangles
above, draw and label a different
rectangle that has either the same
area or the same perimeter.

Name _____ **Date** _____

Class Activity

► **Perimeter of a Parallelogram**

Vocabulary

parallelogram
base
slant height
rhombus

In this **parallelogram**, *b* is the length of the **base** and *s* is the **slant height**. Here are three different ways to find the perimeter of the parallelogram.

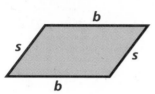

A Add the sides.

$$b + s + b + s = P$$

B Add the length of the base and the length of the slant height. Multiply the total by 2.

$$(b + s) \cdot 2 = P$$

C Multiply the length of the base by 2. Multiply the length of the slant height by 2. Find the total.

$$(b \cdot 2) + (s \cdot 2) = P$$

Answer questions 1–4 on a separate sheet of paper.

1. Why do the equations for rectangles also work for parallelograms?

2. Will equation **A** work for all quadrilaterals? Why or why not?

3. Will equations **B** and **C** work for quadrilaterals that are not parallelograms? Why or why not?

4. How can you change the equations to make them work for a **rhombus**?

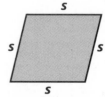

Name _____ **Date** _____

Vocabulary

perpendicular
base
height

▶ Parallelograms and Rectangles

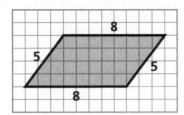

On a sheet of grid paper, draw a parallelogram exactly like the one above. Label the sides with their measurements.

Draw a line segment inside that is **perpendicular** to the **base**.

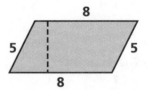

Measure the perpendicular line segment. It is called the **height**.

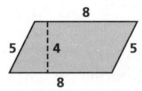

Cut the figure into two pieces along the height.

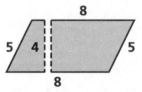

Move the left part over to the right so that the slanting sides touch.

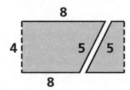

5. What figure did you make? _____

Perimeter and Area of Parallelograms

A–5

Name _____   Date _____

▶ Parallelograms and Rectangles (Continued)

Use your parallelogram to answer the questions.

6. What is the length of the rectangle?

   _____

7. What is the width?

   _____

8. Why can you use the formula for the area of a rectangle
   to find the area of the parallelogram?

   _____

9. Which measurement for the parallelogram do you
   not use to find the area? Why?

   _____

   _____

10. What is the area of the rectangle?

    _____

11. The bottom of a parallelogram is its base (*b*). The height
    (*h*) is perpendicular to the base. What formula can you
    write for the area of a parallelogram?

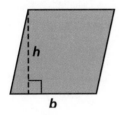

    _____

12. Why does this formula work for both rectangles and
    parallelograms?

    _____

Going Further

▶ **Change Rectangle Dimensions**

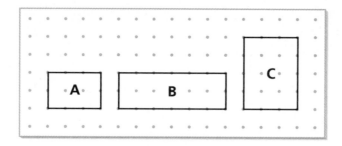

1. Rectangle B is twice as long as Rectangle A. How do their areas compare?

   _____

2. Rectangle C is twice as wide as Rectangle A. How do their areas compare?

   _____

3. What happens to the area when you double one side of the rectangle?

   _____

   _____

4. Draw a rectangle with sides that are double those of Rectangle D.

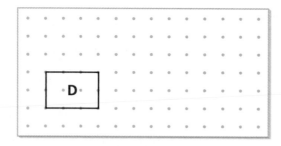

5. What happens to the area when you double both sides of a rectangle?

   _____

   _____

Perimeter and Area of Parallelograms

A–6

Class Activity

Name

Date

Vocabulary

perimeter
area

▶ Explore Complex Figures

City Park has a deep swimming pool for older children. This year the city is planning to add a wading pool for younger children next to the deep pool. In these drawings, the side of each square unit represents 1 yard.

The deep pool: Adding the wading pool: The new pool:

1. What is the shape of the deep pool? _____

2. What are its **perimeter** and **area**? _____

3. What is the shape of the wading pool? _____

4. What are its perimeter and area? _____

5. What is the area of the new pool? _____

6. What is the perimeter of the new pool? _____

7. Why is the area of the new pool the same as the area of the deep pool plus the area of the wading pool?

_____

_____

8. Why is the perimeter of the new pool not the same as the perimeter of the deep pool plus the perimeter of the wading pool?

_____

_____

Class Activity

► Perimeter and Area of Complex Figures

Find the perimeter and area of each figure.

9.   10.

11.

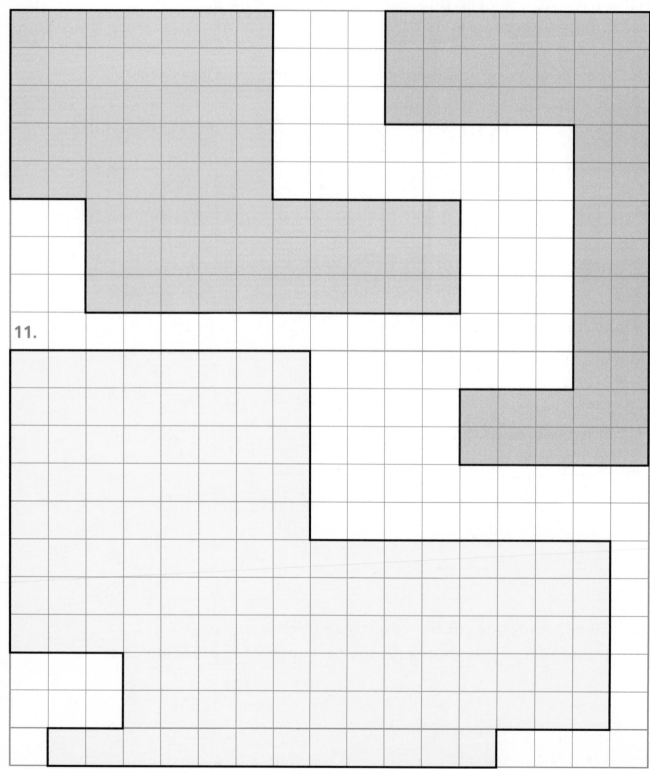

Perimeter and Area of Complex Figures

▶ Perimeter and Area of Complex Figures (Continued)

Find the perimeter of each figure. Then divide each figure into rectangles and find the area. In these drawings, the side of each square unit represents 1 yard.

12.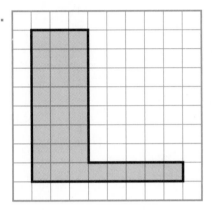

Perimeter: _____

Area: _____

13.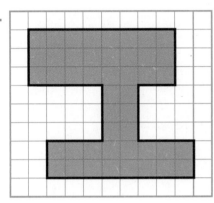

Perimeter: _____

Area: _____

14.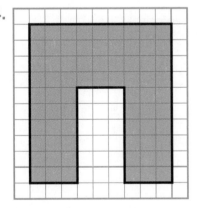

Perimeter: _____

Area: _____

15.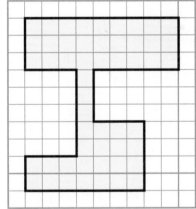

Perimeter: _____

Area: _____

16. Explain Your Thinking Why did you divide figure 12 the way you did?

_____

Vocabulary

dimension

▶ Find the Missing Dimensions

17. Some of the sides in figures A, B, C, and D are not labeled. Write the missing **dimensions**.

A

2 in.

___ in.

5 in.

9 in.   3 in.

___ in.

3 in.

___ in.

B

4 m

4 m   ___ m

3 m   2 m

3 m

2 m   ___ m

___ m   2 m

2 m

C

7 yd

3 yd

3 yd

6 yd

5 yd   ___ yd

___ yd

6 yd

D

10 cm

3 cm

2 cm

4 cm

___ cm   5 cm

4 cm

___ cm

3 cm

___ cm

18. What is the area of each figure?

A _____   B _____   C _____   D _____

19. What is the perimeter of each figure?

A _____   B _____   C _____   D _____

Perimeter and Area of Complex Figures

1. Draw a figure that is congruent to the one shown.

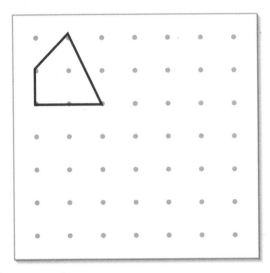

2. Draw all the lines of symmetry for the figure.

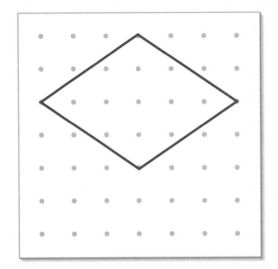

Describe each figure.

3.

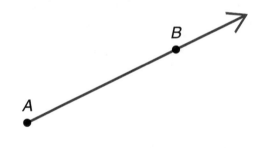

_____

_____

4.

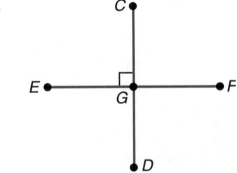

_____

_____

5.

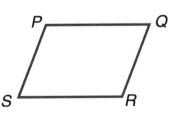

_____

_____

6.

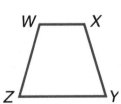

_____

_____

Find the perimeter and area of each figure.
Show your work.

7.

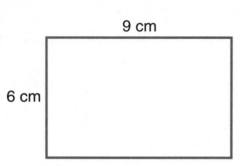

9 cm

6 cm

Perimeter _____

Area _____

8.

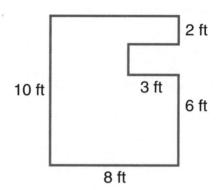

2 ft

10 ft

3 ft

6 ft

8 ft

Perimeter _____

Area _____

Solve each problem.

Show your work.

9. A parallelogram has a base of 10 cm. Its
perimeter is 30 cm. What are the lengths
of the other three sides?

Answer _____

10. **Extended Response** A square has an area of
25 sq ft. What is the length of one side?
Explain your reasoning.

_____

_____

_____

_____

_____

Name _____   Date _____

Vocabulary

Associative Property of Addition

▶ Discuss Addition

Share and explain methods you could use to solve these addition problems.

1. 9 + 6   2. 90 + 60   3. 6 + 7   4. 60 + 70   5. 38 + 6   6. 38 + 56

7. Tell word problems for exercises 1, 2, and 6.

▶ Discuss Subtraction

Share and explain methods you could use to solve these subtraction problems.

8. 15 − 9   9. 150 − 90   10. 13 − 6   11. 130 − 60   12. 44 − 38   13. 94 − 38

14. Tell word problems for exercises 8 and 9.

▶ Add More Than Two Addends

The **Associative Property of Addition** states that grouping the addends in different ways does not change the sum.

$$90 + 10 + 50$$

add 90 + 10 first	add 10 + 50 first
(90 + 10) + 50	90 + (10 + 50)
100 + 50	90 + 60
150 = 150	

Parentheses show you which addends to add first.

15. Use the Associative Property of Addition to show a fast way to find 90 + 40.

_____

_____

16. On the Back Does the Associative Property work for any numbers? Discuss why or why not.

Addition and Subtraction Methods

Dear Family,

Your child is familiar with addition and subtraction problems from past years. Unit 2 of *Math Expressions* guides students as they deepen and extend their mastery of these operations. The main goals of this unit are:

• to help students gain speed and accuracy in addition and subtraction,
• to introduce algebraic expressions and equations that feature these operations,
• to help students see how addition and subtraction relate to real-world situations, and
• to begin exploring two-step problems and mixed word problems.

Your child will learn and practice techniques such as counting on, doubling, regrouping, and ungrouping to gain speed and accuracy in addition and subtraction. Parentheses, which will be used throughout the school year, will be introduced to show which operation should be done first. The symbols "=" and "≠" will be used to show whether numbers and expressions are equal.

Increasing and decreasing change problems will be introduced in which the starting number, the change, or the result will be unknown. Your child will learn how to write an equation to show a change, collection, or comparison situation, and then solve the equation to find the answer to that problem.

Finally, your child will apply this knowledge to solve word problems for which he or she will have to determine the operations needed to solve the problems and carry out a strategy to arrive at a solution.

If you have questions or comments, please contact your child's teacher.

Sincerely,
Your child's teacher

Estimada familia:

Durante los últimos años, su niño se ha familiarizado con problemas de suma y de resta. La Unidad 2 de *Math Expressions* guía a los estudiantes a medida que refuerzan y amplían su habilidad con estas operaciones. Los objetivos principales de esta unidad son:

• ayudar a los estudiantes a adquirir rapidez y exactitud con la suma y la resta,
• presentar expresiones algebraicas y ecuaciones que requieren estas operaciones,
• ayudar a los estudiantes a ver de qué manera la suma y la resta se relacionan con situaciones de la vida real y
• empezar a practicar problemas de dos pasos y problemas verbales mixtos.

Su niño aprenderá y practicará técnicas como contar hacia adelante, duplicar, reagrupar y desagrupar para adquirir rapidez y exactitud con la suma y la resta. A lo largo del año escolar se presentarán los paréntesis, los cuales se usarán para mostrar qué operaciones se deben hacer primero. Los símbolos = y ≠ se usarán para mostrar si los números y expresiones son iguales.

Se presentarán problemas con cambios de aumento o de disminución en los cuales el número inicial, el cambio o el resultado serán desconocidos. Su niño aprenderá a escribir una ecuación para mostrar una situación relacionada con cambio, colección o comparación, y luego a resolver la ecuación y así hallar la respuesta al problema.

Por último, su niño aplicará este conocimiento para resolver problemas verbales, para los que deberá determinar las operaciones necesarias para resolverlos y usar una estrategia para hallar una solución.

Si tiene alguna pregunta o comentario, por favor comuníquese conmigo.

Atentamente,
El maestro de su niño

Addition and Subtraction Methods

Class Activity

Name _____ **Date** _____

Vocabulary

equation
sum
difference

▶ Discuss the = and ≠ Signs

An **equation** is made of two equal quantities or expressions. An equals sign (=) is used to show that the two sides are equal.

$5 = 3 + 2$ $3 + 2 = 5$ $5 = 5$ $3 + 2 = 2 + 3$ $7 - 2 = 1 + 1 + 3$

The "is not equal to" sign (≠) shows that two quantities are not equal.

$4 \neq 3 + 2$ $5 \neq 3 - 1$ $5 \neq 4$ $3 - 2 \neq 1 + 3$ $3 + 2 \neq 1 + 1 + 2$

An equation can have one or more numbers or letters on each side. A **sum** or **difference** can be written on either side of the equals sign.

1. Use the = sign to write four equations. Vary how many numbers you have on each side of your equations.

_____ _____ _____ _____

2. Use the ≠ sign to write four "is not equal to" statements. Vary how many numbers you have on each side of your ≠ signs.

_____ _____ _____ _____

Write = or ≠ to make each statement true.

3. $5 + 2 + 6$ ___ $6 + 7$ 4. 80 ___ $60 - 20$ 5. 70 ___ $40 + 30$

Class Activity

Vocabulary

Commutative Property of Addition

▶ Discuss the Commutative Property

The **Commutative Property of Addition** states that addition can be done in either order.

6. Does 3 + 2 = 2 + 3? _____
   Tell why or why not.

   _____

   _____

   _____

   _____

   _____

7. Does $a + b = b + a$ for any two whole numbers? _____
   Tell why or why not.

   _____

   _____

   _____

8. Does the Commutative Property work for
   subtraction? _____
   Is 3 − 2 = 2 − 3 a true statement? _____
   Tell why or why not.

   _____

   _____

   _____

Understand Equality

Class Activity

Vocabulary

inverse operations
addend

► **Discuss Inverse Operations**

In addition you put two groups together. In subtraction you find an unknown addend or take away one group. Addition and subtraction are **inverse operations**. They undo each other.

Addends are numbers that are added to make a sum. You can find two addends of a number by breaking apart the number.

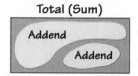

Total (Sum)

Addend
Addend

A break-apart drawing can help you find all eight related addition and subtraction equations for two addends.

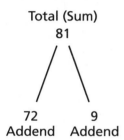

Total (Sum)
81

72   9
Addend   Addend

$81 = 72 + 9$ $72 + 9 = 81$

$81 = 9 + 72$ $9 + 72 = 81$

$72 = 81 - 9$ $81 - 9 = 72$

$9 = 81 - 72$ $81 - 72 = 9$

9. Which equations show the Commutative Property?

_____

10. Circle the total in each equation. Where is the total in a subtraction equation?

_____

Solve each equation.

11. $50 = 30 + p$

$p =$ _____

12. $q + 20 = 60$

$q =$ _____

13. $90 - v = 50$

$v =$ _____

14. Write the eight related addition and subtraction equations for the break-apart drawing.

56

48   8

_____   _____

_____   _____

_____   _____

_____   _____

Going Further

Vocabulary

inequality

▶ Inequalities

A number sentence that shows that two amounts are not equal is an **inequality**. The "greater than" sign (>) shows that the quantity on the left is greater than the quantity on the right.

$$9 > 3 \qquad 6 > 0 \qquad 2 + 8 > 7$$

The "less than" sign (<) shows that the quantity on the left is less than the quantity on the right.

$$5 < 7 \qquad 0 < 1 \qquad 8 - 4 < 6$$

Write > or < to make each statement true.

1. 16 ___ 18

2. 55 ___ 47

3. 5 + 2 ___ 9

4. 25 + 15 ___ 35

5. 9 + 2 ___ 3 + 4 + 1

6. 120 ___ 84 + 44

Write + or − to make each statement true.

7. 5 ___ 2 < 6

8. 12 > 9 ___ 4

9. 8 ___ 7 > 13

10. 11 ___ 6 > 8

11. 22 ___ 9 < 19

12. 7 + 3 < 6 ___ 5

Write four numbers. Then write three different inequalities, using all four numbers in each inequality.

_____

_____

_____

_____

Class Activity

Vocabulary
situation equation
solution equation

▶ Discuss Change Problems

Change Situations	
Change Plus:	Start + Change = Result
Change Minus:	Start − Change = Result

Read each problem and discuss the equations.

A. At the park, 6 children were playing. Some more children came to the park. Now, 13 children are at the park. How many more children came to the park?
Situation Equation: $6 + c = 13$
Solution Equation: $13 - 6 = c$

B. At the park, some children were playing. Then 20 children had to go home. Now 30 children are left. How many children were at the park first?
Situation Equation: $p - 20 = 30$
Solution Equation: $20 + 30 = p$

▶ Solve Change Problems

Show your work.

Write a situation equation or a solution equation using a letter to represent the unknown. Make a math drawing if you need to.

1. One afternoon, 63 books were checked out of a library. That day, 72 books in all were checked out. How many books were checked out that morning?

_____

_____

2. At noon, 70 students went to the school cafeteria for lunch. After 15 minutes, only 19 of those students remained. How many students left the cafeteria during that time?

_____

_____

Class Activity

Vocabulary

change plus
change minus

▶ Write Change Problems

Choose 2 equations. Write a change plus or a change minus word problem to represent each situation equation.

$$35 + n = 40 \qquad n - 20 = 5 \qquad 5 + 40 = n$$

$$n + 40 = 45 \qquad 45 - n = 20 \qquad 50 - 5 = n$$

3. _____

_____

_____

_____

_____

_____

_____

_____

4. _____

_____

_____

_____

_____

_____

_____

_____

Vocabulary

Collection Situations

▶ Discuss Collection Problems

Collection situations involve a total amount broken into two addends. There are three kinds of collection situations.

No Action: The problem describes the total and the addends.

Put Together: The two addends are put together to make the total.

Take Apart: The total is taken apart to make the two addends.

Collection situations can have an unknown total or an unknown addend (partner). You can use a break-apart drawing to relate the addends and the total. Or you can write a situation or solution equation.

1. Elizabeth's mother picked 9 blue flowers and 7 red flowers. How many flowers did Elizabeth's mother pick?

2. A fruit bowl contains 18 pieces of fruit. Of these, 13 are apples and the rest are bananas. How many bananas are in the bowl?

Break-Apart Drawings

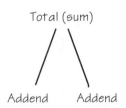

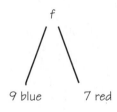

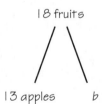

Situation Equations: $f = 9 + 7$ $18 = 13 + b$

Solution Equations: $9 + 7 = f$ $18 - 13 = b$ or $13 + b = 18$

▶ Solve Collection Problems

Make a break-apart drawing for each problem. Then write and solve an equation using a letter to represent the unknown.

Show your work.

3. A stamp collection contains 90 domestic stamps and 40 foreign stamps. How many stamps does the collection contain altogether?

_____

4. The enrollment in a small middle school is 130 students. Of those students, 70 are girls. How many students in the school are boys?

_____

5. A school has 110 folding chairs. Some chairs are in storage and the other 80 chairs are in the auditorium. How many chairs are in storage?

_____

6. Noreen put $10 in her pocket and the other $35 in her wallet. How much money does Noreen have?

_____

7. The 1:00 P.M. showing of a movie had 50 adults and 60 children in the audience. How many people attended the movie?

_____

8. In a collection of 200 coins, 20 coins are pennies. How many coins in the collection are not pennies?

_____

Class Activity

▶ Write the Appropriate Label

Write a label to complete each answer.

9. 9 adults + 5 children = 14 _____

10. 7 dimes + 1 penny = 8 _____

11. 8 apples + 8 oranges = 16 _____

12. 4 cats + 6 dogs = 10 _____

▶ Break-Apart Drawings

Write a collection problem for each break-apart drawing.
Then solve the problems.

13.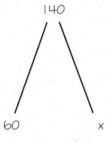

140

60   x

_____

_____

_____

_____

_____

_____

14.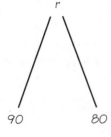

r

90   80

_____

_____

_____

_____

_____

_____

 15. On the Back Make a break-apart drawing. Then write
and solve a problem using your drawing.

Addition and Subtraction Collection Problems

Class Activity

Vocabulary
comparison situations
difference
comparison bars

▶ Discuss Comparison Situations

In Unit 1, you learned about multiplication and division **comparison situations**. You can also compare by addition and subtraction. You can find *how much more* or *how much less* one amount is than another.

The amount more or less is called the **difference**. In some problems, the difference is not given. You have to find it. In other problems, the smaller or the larger amount is not given.

Mai has 9 apples and 12 plums.

- How many more plums than apples does she have?
- How many fewer apples than plums does she have?

Plums

| 12 |

Apples

| 9 | (d)

Comparison bars can help us show which is more. We show the difference in an oval.

Draw comparison bars for each problem. Write and solve an equation. Discuss other equations you could use.

1. The nursery has 70 rose bushes and 50 tea tree bushes. How many fewer tea tree bushes than rose bushes are at the nursery?

2. Dan wants to plant 30 trees. He has dug 21 holes. How many trees don't have a hole yet?

Class Activity

Vocabulary

leading
misleading

▶ **Discuss the Language**

The large amount or the small amount can be the unknown. Some comparing sentences have **leading** language that suggests what to do. Other comparing sentences have **misleading** language that may trick you into doing the wrong operation.

Fill in and label the comparison bars and solve. Say the reverse comparing sentence to see if it helps you.

3. There are 10 dogs at the kennel. There are 6 fewer dogs than cats. How many cats are at the kennel?

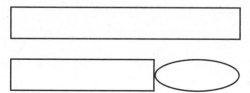

_____

4. There are 15 girls in Ms. Roedel's fourth-grade class. There are 3 more girls than boys. How many boys are there?

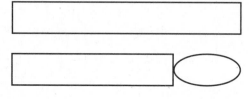

_____

Class Activity

▶ Share Solutions

Draw comparison bars for each problem. Write and solve an equation. Don't let misleading language trick you!

Show your work.

5. At the zoo there are 7 monkeys. There are 6 more kangaroos than monkeys. How many kangaroos are at the zoo?

_____

6. The soccer team drilled for 50 minutes. It drilled 10 minutes longer than it scrimmaged. How long did the soccer team scrimmage?

_____

7. Avery is 13 years old. He is 4 years older than Marisa. How old is Marisa?

_____

8. Sabrina studied 15 more minutes than Sean. How long did Sean study if Sabrina studied for 45 minutes?

_____

9. On the last day of school, 10 more students wore shorts than wore jeans. If 13 students wore jeans, how many students wore shorts?

_____

10. **On the Back** Write a comparison problem. Show comparison bars and an equation to solve your problem.

Addition and Subtraction Comparison Problems

Class Activity

▶ Discuss the Steps of the Problem

Sometimes you will need to work through more than one step to solve a problem. The steps can be shown in one or more equations.

1. In the morning, 19 students were working on a science project. In the afternoon, 3 students left and 7 more students came to work on the project. How many students were working on the project at the end of the day?

   _____

2. Solve the problem again by finishing Tommy's and Lucy's methods. Then discuss what is alike and what is different about each method.

Tommy's Method	Lucy's Method
Write an equation for each step.	**Write an equation for the whole problem.**
Find the total number of students who worked on the project.	Let n = the number of students working on the project at the end of the day.
$19 + 7 = $ _____	Students who left in the afternoon. Students who arrived in the afternoon.
Subtract the number of students who left in the afternoon.	
$26 - 3 = $ _____	$19 - $ _____ $ + $ _____ $ = n$
	_____ $= n$

3. Solve. Discuss the steps you used.

   A team is scheduled to play 12 games. Of those games, 7 will be played at home. The other games are away games. How many fewer away games than home games will be played?

   _____

   _____

▶ Share Solutions

Solve each problem mentally or use equations, comparison bars, or break-apart drawings.

Show your work.

4. A garden contains 54 vegetable plants. Altogether, the garden has 63 fruit and vegetable plants. How many fewer fruit plants than vegetable plants are there?

_____

_____

5. Tyler is thinking of a number. If 5 is added to his number and 8 is subtracted from the total, the result is 2. What is Tyler's number?

_____

6. At the end of the school day, 8 of 17 students in a class rode the bus home. How many fewer students rode the bus home than did not ride the bus home?

_____

7. Zara has 4 pencils, 2 pens, 12 markers, and 24 crayons. How many more markers than pencils and pens does Zara have?

_____

_____

8. Hannah studied for 40 minutes on the evening before a test. On the day of the test, she studied for 15 minutes before school and for 10 minutes after lunch. Did Hannah study for more than one hour? Explain your answer.

_____

_____

Name _____ **Date** _____

Class Activity

▶ Discuss Types of Problems

Addition and Subtraction Situations

Addition and subtraction problems involve two **addends** and a **total**. Either the total or one addend will be unknown.

1. Hassan had 5 marbles. Jenny gave him more marbles. Now Hassan has 14 marbles. How many marbles did Jenny give Hassan?

   _____

2. After spending 40¢, Michael has 6 dimes. How much money did he start with?

   _____

3. Eliza has $15. This amount is $7 less than she had yesterday. How much money did Eliza have yesterday?

   _____

4. The school has 20 windows open. There are 50 windows altogether. How many windows are closed?

   _____

Multiplication and Division Situations

Multiplication and division involve repeated groups of the same size.

5. Jevon has 30 trading cards. He has 3 times as many as Ramon. How many trading cards does Ramon have?

   _____

   Do you need to multiply or divide to solve this problem?

   _____

6. Jenita had 5 baskets of apples with 10 apples in each basket. She gave away 2 baskets. How many apples does she have now?

   _____

   What operations do you need to do to solve this problem?

   _____

▶ Share Solutions

Solve.

Show your work.

7. A math test was given to 26 students. After 20 minutes, 9 students had completed the test. What number of students took more than 20 minutes to complete the test?

   _____

8. Anna spent $18 for a pair of jeans and had $32 left over. How much money did Anna have before she bought the jeans?

   _____

9. A class has 24 students. The teacher wants to make 3 math teams with the same number of students on each team. How many students will be on each team?

   _____

10. Jason receives five dollars each week for his allowance. His older brother gets 3 times as much as Jason. How much does Jason's older brother get after two weeks?

    _____

11. The faculty of a school is made up of 17 female teachers. There are 2 more female teachers than male teachers. How many teachers are at the school altogether?

    _____

12. A box contains 60 oranges. A basket contains $\frac{1}{3}$ as many apples as oranges. How many apples are in the basket?

    _____

Mixed Word Problems

Class Activity

Name _____

Date _____

Vocabulary
dot array
place-value drawings

▶ Represent Hundreds

You can represent numbers by making **place-value drawings** on a **dot array**.

1. What number does this drawing show? _____
   Explain your thinking.

   _____

   _____

▶ Represent Thousands

Discuss this place-value drawing. Write the number of each.

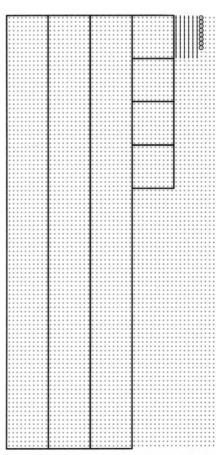

2. ones: _____

3. quick tens: _____

4. hundred boxes: _____

5. thousand bars: _____

6. How many hundred boxes could we draw inside each thousand bar? Explain.

   _____

   _____

7. What number does this drawing show?

   _____

▶ Draw Larger Numbers

Place value can also be shown without using a dot array.

8. What number does this drawing represent?
Explain your thinking.

_____

_____

_____

_____

What would the drawing represent if it had:

9. 3 more hundred boxes? _____

10. 0 hundred boxes? _____

11. 2 fewer quick tens? _____

12. 2 more quick tens? _____

13. 0 quick tens? _____

14. 5 fewer ones? _____

15. 0 ones? _____

16. 4 more thousand bars? _____

17. On your MathBoard, make a place-value drawing for a different number that has the digits 1, 2, 7, and 9.

18. Explain how your drawing is similar to and different from the drawing for 1,279.

_____

_____

Place Value to Thousands

▶ Practice With Place-Value Drawings

Make a place-value drawing for each number, using ones, quick tens, hundred boxes, and thousand bars.

19. 6

20. 3

21. 603

22. 300

23. 63

24. 32

25. 325

26. 3,285

27. 109

28. 573

Going Further

Name _____ Date _____

► Place Value and Money

Mr. Jansen wants to buy a television for $214. He doesn't have 214 dollar bills in his pocket! What bills can Mr. Jansen use to pay for the television?

We can use place value to see how Mr. Jansen can pay for the television.

214 = 200 + 10 + 4
$214 = $200 + $10 + $4

Mr. Jansen can use 2 hundred-dollar bills, 1 ten-dollar bill, and 4 one-dollar bills to pay for the television.

Write the amount shown.

1. 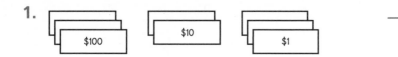 _____

2. 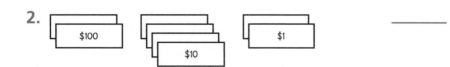 _____

3. 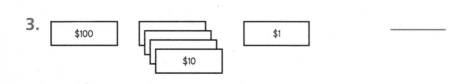 _____

4. Ron deposited 7 hundred-dollar bills and 6 one-dollar bills into his bank account. Write the amount he deposited.

_____

5. Fran has 3 hundred-dollar bills, 8 ten-dollar bills, and 20 one-dollar bills. What is the fewest number of bills she could receive in exchange?

_____

Place Value to Thousands

Dear Family,

Beginning today, your child will be learning about place values in our number system and about how to read and write large numbers. In a few days, your child will learn about addition with large numbers. An important concept is that we need to add digits with the same place value. We must add ones to ones, tens to tens, and so on. The *Math Expressions* program encourages children to think about "making new groups" to help them understand place values.

We call the addition method below "New Groups Above" because the numbers that represent the new groups are written above the problem.

1. Add the ones:
5 + 7 = 12 ones
12 = 2 ones + 10 ones, and 10 ones = 1 new ten.

2. Add the tens:
1 + 7 + 6 = 14 tens
14 = 4 tens + 10 tens, and 10 tens = 1 new hundred.

3. Add the hundreds:
1 + 1 = 2 hundreds

Step 2 is harder because you need to add the 1 to 7 and remember 8 and then add 8 and 6.

$$\begin{array}{r} (1) \\ 175 \\ + 67 \\ \hline 2 \end{array}$$

$$\begin{array}{r} (1)1 \\ 175 \\ + 67 \\ \hline 42 \end{array}$$

$$\begin{array}{r} 11 \\ 175 \\ + 67 \\ \hline 242 \end{array}$$

We call the following method "New Groups Below." The steps are the same as those above, but the new groups are written below the addends.

It is easier to see the totals for each column (12 and 14) and adding is easier because you add the two numbers you see and then add the 1 (7 + 6 + 1).

1.
$$\begin{array}{r} 175 \\ + 67 \\ \hline 2 \end{array}$$

2.
$$\begin{array}{r} 175 \\ + 67 \\ \hline 42 \end{array}$$

3.
$$\begin{array}{r} 175 \\ + 67 \\ \hline 242 \end{array}$$

It is important that your child maintain his or her home practice with basic multiplication and division. If you need practice items or materials, please contact me.

Sincerely,
Your child's teacher

Estimada familia:

A partir de hoy, su niño aprenderá los valores posicionales de nuestro sistema numérico, y a leer y escribir números grandes. Dentro de unos días, su niño aprenderá a sumar números grandes. Un concepto importante es que debemos sumar dígitos del mismo valor posicional. Debemos sumar unidades con unidades, decenas con decenas, y así sucesivamente. El programa *Math Expressions* anima a los niños a pensar en "hacer grupos nuevos" para ayudarlos a comprender los valores posicionales.

El método de suma que se muestra se llama "Grupos nuevos arriba" porque los números que representan los grupos nuevos se escriben arriba del problema.

1. Suma las unidades:
5 + 7 = 12 unidades
12 = 2 unidades
+ 10 unidades,
y 10 unidades =
1 nueva decena.

2. Suma las decenas:
1 + 7 + 6 = 14 decenas
14 = 4 decenas
+ 10 decenas,
y 10 decenas =
1 nueva centena.

3. Suma las centenas:
1 + 1 = 2 centenas

El paso 2 es más difícil porque hay que sumar el 1 al 7, recordar el 8 y luego sumar 8 + 6.

$$
\begin{array}{r}
\overset{(1)}{175} \\
+\ 67 \\
\hline
2
\end{array}
\qquad
\begin{array}{r}
\overset{(1)}{1}\overset{1}{75} \\
+\ 67 \\
\hline
42
\end{array}
\qquad
\begin{array}{r}
\overset{1}{1}\overset{1}{75} \\
+\ 67 \\
\hline
242
\end{array}
$$

Al siguiente método le damos el nombre de "Grupos nuevos abajo".

Es más fácil ver los totales de cada columna (12 y 14) y sumar porque sumas los dos números que ves, y luego sumas 1 (7 + 6 + 1).

$$
\textbf{1.}\quad
\begin{array}{r}
175 \\
+\ 67 \\
\hline
2
\end{array}
\qquad
\textbf{2.}\quad
\begin{array}{r}
175 \\
+\ 67 \\
\hline
42
\end{array}
\qquad
\textbf{3.}\quad
\begin{array}{r}
175 \\
+\ 67 \\
\hline
242
\end{array}
$$

Es importante que su niño siga practicando las multiplicaciones y divisiones básicas en casa. Si usted necesita elementos o materiales para practicar, por favor comuníquese conmigo.

Atentamente,
El maestro de su niño

Place Value to Thousands

Class Activity

Thousands	Hundreds	Tens	Ones
__, 0 0 0	__0 0	__0	__
__, 0 0 0	__0 0	__0	__
__, 0 0 0	__0 0	__0	__
__, 0 0 0	__0 0	__0	__
__, 0 0 0	__0 0	__0	__
__, 0 0 0	__0 0	__0	__
__, 0 0 0	__0 0	__0	__
__, 0 0 0	__0 0	__0	__

Name _____ **Date** _____

Class Activity

▶ Write Numbers Different Ways

Standard form: 261

Word form: Two hundred sixty-one

Place-value words: 2 hundreds 6 tens 1 one

Write each number in standard form and using place-value words.

1. thirty-five

_____

2. three hundred five

_____

3. three hundred fifty

_____

4. three hundred fifteen

_____

5. six thousand, eight

_____

6. six thousand, one hundred eight

_____

Write the value of the underlined digit.

7. 7$\underline{5}$6 _____

8. $\underline{4}$,831 _____

9. 6,$\underline{5}$07 _____

▶ Round Numbers

Round to the nearest ten. Make a rounding frame for the first number.

10. $\overline{87}$

11. 17 _____

12. 34 _____

13. 71 _____

14. 65 _____

Round to the nearest hundred. Make a rounding frame for the first number.

15. $\overline{734}$

16. 363 _____

17. 158 _____

Round each number to the nearest thousand. Make a rounding frame for the first number.

18. $\overline{1,275}$

19. 8,655 _____

20. 5,182 _____

Name _____ **Date** _____

Going Further

▶ Expanded Form

Another way to write numbers is using **expanded form**.

Standard form: 8,562

Word form: Eight thousand, five hundred sixty-two

Expanded form: 8,000 + 500 + 60 + 2

Write each number in expanded form.

1. 7,834 _____

2. 906 _____

3. 8,083 _____

4. 1,060 _____

5. 450 _____

6. 1,006 _____

7. 5,108 _____

8. 6,019 _____

9. 2,727 _____

10. 444 _____

Write each number in standard form.

11. 900 + 20 + 5 _____

12. 4,000 + 500 + 70 _____

13. 3,000 + 600 + 9 _____

14. 7,000 + 90 + 3 _____

15. 8,000 + 70 + 6 _____

16. 100 + 30 + 1 _____

17. 2,000 + 300 _____

18. 6,000 + 800 + 4 _____

19. 2,000 + 1 _____

20. 6,000 + 80 + 4 _____

Write each number in word form.

21. 400 + 30 + 7 _____

22. 5,000 + 300 _____

23. 600 + 10 + 3 _____

24. 1,000 + 5 _____

Read, Write, and Round Numbers

Name _____ **Date** _____

Vocabulary

greater than >
less than <
digit

▶ Compare Numbers

Discuss the problem below.

Jim has 24 trading cards and Hattie has 42 trading cards. Who has more trading cards? How do you know?

Write > (greater than), < (less than), or = to make each statement true.

1. 26 _____ 29

2. 44 _____ 34

3. 26 _____ 62

4. 74 _____ 77

5. 85 _____ 58

6. 126 _____ 162

7. 253 _____ 235

8. 620 _____ 602

9. 825 _____ 528

10. 478 _____ 488

11. 3,294 _____ 3,924

12. 8,925 _____ 9,825

13. 6,706 _____ 6,760

14. 4,106 _____ 4,016

15. 1,997 _____ 1,799

▶ Greatest and Least

Write the *greatest* and the *least* four-digit number possible. Use each of the 4 digits in the group exactly once.

16. 6, 3, 8, 2

Greatest _____

Least _____

17. 4, 9, 1, 5

Greatest _____

Least _____

18. 0, 6, 7, 3

Greatest _____

Least _____

19. 0, 4, 0, 1

Greatest _____

Least _____

Class Activity

Name _____ **Date** _____

▶ Use a Number Line

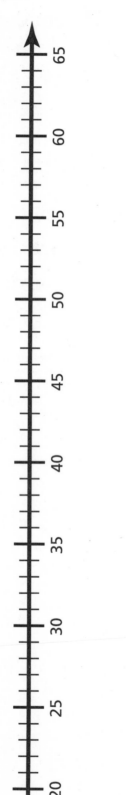

A 20 25 30 35 40 45 50 55 60 65

B 100 110 120 130 140 150 160 170 180 190

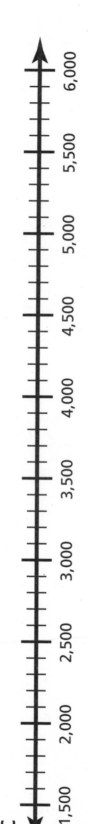

C 1,500 2,000 2,500 3,000 3,500 4,000 4,500 5,000 5,500 6,000

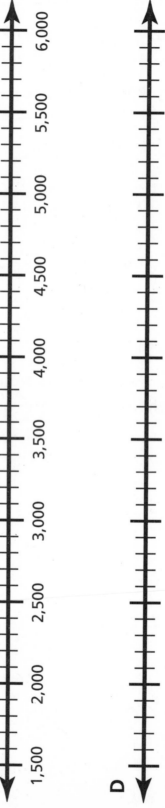

D

E

Compare Whole Numbers

Vocabulary

greatest
least

▶ Compare Numbers on a Number Line

The range of numbers that fall between 25 and 55 does not include the numbers 25 and 55.

20. Circle the numbers 25 and 55 on the number line below.

21. Shade the range of numbers between 25 and 55.

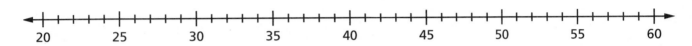

22. Put Xs on 27 and 57. Are both 27 and 57 within the range 25 to 55?

_____

23. Think about the number range 110 to 190. Are both 117 and 171 within the range? Explain how you know.

_____

24. Think about the number range 1,500 to 1,700. Are both 1,705 and 1,507 within the range? Explain how you know.

_____

▶ Ordering Numbers

Write each group of numbers in order from greatest to least. Then tell whether the first or last number is closer to the middle number.

25. 20, 10, 29

_____

_____

26. 68, 75, 60

_____

_____

27. 120, 100, 200

_____

_____

Going Further

Name _____

Date _____

▶ Compare Expressions

Expressions can be compared using the "greater than" sign (>), the "less than" sign (<), or the "equals" sign (=).

$$9 - 6 < 1 + 3 \qquad 1 \times 5 > 0 \times 5 \qquad 8 - 4 = 12 \div 3$$

Simplify each expression. Then, write >, <, or = to make each statement true.

1. $6 \times 3 \bigcirc 6 + 3$ 2. $16 - 5 \bigcirc 9 + 4$ 3. $4 \times 2 \bigcirc 54 \div 6$

4. $25 \div 5 \bigcirc 5 \times 1$ 5. $5 + 2 \bigcirc 1 \times 4$ 6. $9 - 5 \bigcirc 32 \div 4$

7. $19 - 18 \bigcirc 4 \times 4$ 8. $12 - 4 \bigcirc 24 \div 6$ 9. $8 + 7 \bigcirc 56 \div 7$

10. $11 + 5 \bigcirc 6 \times 2$ 11. $2 \times 2 \bigcirc 45 \div 9$ 12. $7 + 3 \bigcirc 5 \times 2$

Write numbers to make true statements.

13. ___ + ___ < ___ − ___

14. ___ ÷ ___ > ___ × ___

15. ___ − ___ < ___ ÷ ___

16. ___ × ___ > ___ − ___

You can make **inequality** chains using > or <.

$$3 + 5 < 10 - 1 < 40 \div 4$$

Write some inequality chains of your own.

_____

_____

_____

_____

_____

_____

Compare Whole Numbers

Vocabulary

place value

► Identify Place Value

To read and write numbers, you need to understand **place value**.

1. What are the names of the places of a 3-digit number?

_____

Hundreds	Tens	Ones
2	3	5

2. How do we read and write 235 with words?

_____

Hundred Thousands	Ten Thousands	Thousands	,	Hundreds	Tens	Ones
4	6	8	,	2	3	5

3. Read the number 8,235. Then write 8,235 using words.

_____

_____

4. Read the number 68,235. Then write 68,235 using words.

_____

_____

5. Read the number 468,235. Then write 468,235 using words.

_____

Hundred Millions	Ten Millions	Millions	,	Hundred Thousands	Ten Thousands	Thousands	,	Hundreds	Tens	Ones
1	7	9	,	4	6	8	,	2	3	5

6. Read the number 9,468,235. Then write 9,468,235 using words.

_____

_____

7. Read the number 79,468,235. Then write it using words.

_____

_____

8. Read the number 179,468,235. Then write it using words.

_____

Class Activity

▶ Read and Write Large Numbers

Read each number aloud.

9. 39,012   10. 5,709,812   11. 640,739,812   12. 358,917,426

13. 102,453,068   14. 460,053,105   15. 297,365,004   16. 862,050,139

Write each number in words.

17. 9,802

_____

18. 730,812

_____

19. 45,039,812

_____

20. 521,600,439

_____

Write each number in standard form.

21. two thousand, fifty-three

_____

22. one hundred forty thousand, one hundred four

_____

23. seventy-six thousand, five

_____

24. three million, fifty-nine thousand, two hundred sixty-one

_____

25. seven hundred thousand, four hundred thirty

_____

26. four hundred eighty-six million, thirty-one thousand, two hundred seventy-nine

_____

Numbers to Millions

▶ Build a Million

▶ Discuss Different Methods

Discuss how each part of the place-value drawing is related to each addition method.

879

+

754

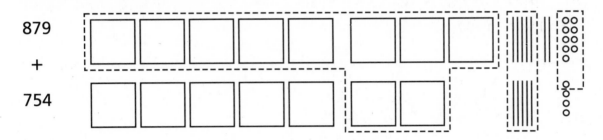

1. New Groups Above Method

Step 1	Step 2	Step 3
1	1 1	1 1
879	879	879
+ 754	+ 754	+ 754
3	33	1,633

2. New Groups Below Method

Step 1	Step 2	Step 3
879	879	879
+ 754	+ 754	+ 754
1	1 1	1 1
3	33	1,633

3. Show Subtotals Method   Left-to-Right   Right-to-Left

Step 1	Step 2	Step 3	Step 4	
879	879	879	879	879
+ 754	+ 754	+ 754	+ 754	+ 754
1,500	1,500	1,500	1,500	13
	120	120	120	120
		13	+ 13	+ 1,500
			1,633	1,633

4. Discuss how each method above shows new groups.

5. On a separate sheet of paper, describe how the Left-to-Right solution and the Right-to-Left solution are alike and how they are different.

Name   **Date**

Going Further

▶ Addition and Money

You can use models to help you add money amounts.

Carlos is saving money to buy a skateboard. He saved $27
one week and $14 the next week.

To find how much he saved altogether, use play money to act out the problem.

Use play money to solve each problem.

Show your work.

1. Robyn's grandmother gave her $38 for her birthday
   and her uncle gave her $25. How much did Robyn
   get altogether?

   _____

2. Melise's family bought a table for $264 and a chair
   for $172. How much did the family pay for the table
   and chair together?

   _____

3. A parent-teacher club sold baked goods to raise
   money for the school. They collected $268 on Friday
   and $479 on Saturday. How much did they collect
   altogether?

   _____

Make New Groups for Addition

Class Activity

Name _____ Date _____

► Analyze Different Methods

New Groups Above

Step 1
$$\begin{array}{r} \overset{1}{} \\ 56{,}973{,}608 \\ +\ 8{,}591{,}729 \\ \hline 7 \end{array}$$

Step 2
$$\begin{array}{r} \overset{1}{} \\ 56{,}973{,}608 \\ +\ 8{,}591{,}729 \\ \hline 37 \end{array}$$

Step 3
$$\begin{array}{r} \overset{1}{} \\ 56{,}973{,}608 \\ +\ 8{,}591{,}729 \\ \hline 337 \end{array}$$

Step 4
$$\begin{array}{r} \overset{1}{} \\ 56{,}973{,}608 \\ +\ 8{,}591{,}729 \\ \hline 5{,}337 \end{array}$$

Step 5
$$\begin{array}{r} \overset{1}{} \\ 56{,}973{,}608 \\ +\ 8{,}591{,}729 \\ \hline 65{,}337 \end{array}$$

Step 6
$$\begin{array}{r} \overset{1\ 1\ 1}{} \\ 56{,}973{,}608 \\ +\ 8{,}591{,}729 \\ \hline 565{,}337 \end{array}$$

Step 7
$$\begin{array}{r} \overset{1\ 1\ 1\ 1}{} \\ 56{,}973{,}608 \\ +\ 8{,}591{,}729 \\ \hline 5{,}565{,}337 \end{array}$$

Step 8
$$\begin{array}{r} \overset{1\ 1\ 1\ 1}{} \\ 56{,}973{,}608 \\ +\ 8{,}591{,}729 \\ \hline 65{,}565{,}337 \end{array}$$

New Groups Below

Step 1
$$\begin{array}{r} 56{,}973{,}608 \\ +\ 8{,}591{,}729 \\ \hline \underset{1}{7} \end{array}$$

Step 2
$$\begin{array}{r} 56{,}973{,}608 \\ +\ 8{,}591{,}729 \\ \hline \underset{1}{37} \end{array}$$

Step 3
$$\begin{array}{r} 56{,}973{,}608 \\ +\ 8{,}591{,}729 \\ \hline 337 \end{array}$$

Step 4
$$\begin{array}{r} 56{,}973{,}608 \\ +\ 8{,}591{,}729 \\ \hline 5{,}337 \end{array}$$

Step 5
$$\begin{array}{r} 56{,}973{,}608 \\ +\ 8{,}591{,}729 \\ \hline 65{,}337 \end{array}$$

Step 6
$$\begin{array}{r} 56{,}973{,}608 \\ +\ 8{,}591{,}729 \\ \hline 565{,}337 \end{array}$$

Step 7
$$\begin{array}{r} 56{,}973{,}608 \\ +\ 8{,}591{,}729 \\ \hline 5{,}565{,}337 \end{array}$$

Step 8
$$\begin{array}{r} 56{,}973{,}608 \\ +\ 8{,}591{,}729 \\ \hline 65{,}565{,}337 \end{array}$$

Show Subtotals (Left-to-Right)

Step 1
$$\begin{array}{r} 56{,}973{,}608 \\ +\ 8{,}591{,}729 \\ \hline 50{,}000{,}000 \end{array}$$

Step 2
$$\begin{array}{r} 56{,}973{,}608 \\ +\ 8{,}591{,}729 \\ \hline 50{,}000{,}000 \\ 14{,}000{,}000 \end{array}$$

Step 3
$$\begin{array}{r} 56{,}973{,}608 \\ +\ 8{,}591{,}729 \\ \hline 50{,}000{,}000 \\ 14{,}000{,}000 \\ 1{,}400{,}000 \end{array}$$

Step 4
$$\begin{array}{r} 56{,}973{,}608 \\ +\ 8{,}591{,}729 \\ \hline 50{,}000{,}000 \\ 14{,}000{,}000 \\ 1{,}400{,}000 \\ 160{,}000 \end{array}$$

Step 5
$$\begin{array}{r} 56{,}973{,}608 \\ +\ 8{,}591{,}729 \\ \hline 50{,}000{,}000 \\ 14{,}000{,}000 \\ 1{,}400{,}000 \\ 160{,}000 \\ 4{,}000 \end{array}$$

Step 6
$$\begin{array}{r} 56{,}973{,}608 \\ +\ 8{,}591{,}729 \\ \hline 50{,}000{,}000 \\ 14{,}000{,}000 \\ 1{,}400{,}000 \\ 160{,}000 \\ 4{,}000 \\ 1{,}300 \end{array}$$

Steps 7 & 8
$$\begin{array}{r} 56{,}973{,}608 \\ +\ 8{,}591{,}729 \\ \hline 50{,}000{,}000 \\ 14{,}000{,}000 \\ 1{,}400{,}000 \\ 160{,}000 \\ 4{,}000 \\ 1{,}300 \\ 20 \\ 17 \end{array}$$

Step 9
$$\begin{array}{r} 56{,}973{,}608 \\ +\ 8{,}591{,}729 \\ \hline 50{,}000{,}000 \\ 14{,}000{,}000 \\ 1{,}400{,}000 \\ 160{,}000 \\ 4{,}000 \\ 1{,}300 \\ 20 \\ +\ 17 \\ \hline 65{,}565{,}337 \end{array}$$

Class Activity

Name _____ **Date** _____

Vocabulary

digit

▶ Find the Mistake

When you add, it is important that you add **digits** in like places.

Look at the these addition exercises.

43,629 + 5,807   1,468 + 327,509   8,570,952 + 4,306

$$\begin{array}{r} 43,629 \\ + \ 5,807 \\ \hline 101,699 \end{array} \qquad \begin{array}{r} 1,468 \\ + \ 327,509 \\ \hline 474,309 \end{array} \qquad \begin{array}{r} 8,570,952 \\ + \ 4,306 \\ \hline 9,001,552 \end{array}$$

1. What mistake appears in all three exercises above?

_____

_____

▶ Practice Aligning Places

**Copy each exercise, lining up places correctly. Then add.
Show your new groups.**

2. 2,647 + 38 = _____   3. 156 + 83,291 = _____

4. 4,389 + 49,706 = _____   5. 135,826 + 2,927 = _____

6. 2,347,092 + 6,739 = _____   7. 15,231 + 57,697,084 = _____

8. Write an addition word problem that has an answer of $43,568.

_____

_____

_____

_____

_____

_____

Addition to Millions

Name _____ **Date** _____

Class Activity

▶ Use Estimating

You can use rounding to estimate a total. Then you can adjust your estimated total to find the exact total.

The best-selling fruits at Joy's Fruit Shack are peaches and bananas. During one month Joy sold 397 peaches and 412 bananas.

1. *About* how many peaches and bananas did she sell in all?

   _____

2. *Exactly* how many peaches and bananas did she sell?

   _____

Estimate. Then adjust your estimate to find the exact answer.

3. 89 + 28 = _____

4. 153 + 98 = _____

5. 1,297 + 802 = _____

6. 1,066 + 45,104 = _____

Solve.

Show your work.

Tomás has $20.00 for some toys. The 3 toys he wants cost $3.98, $4.95, and $2.85. He also wants to buy 2 action figures that are 2 for $7.50.

7. How can Tomás figure out whether he has enough money for all five items? Does he have enough?

   _____

   _____

8. Explain how he can figure out how much change he should get.

   _____

   _____

Name _____

Date _____

▶ Use Estimating (Continued)

Solve.

Mack has $5.00 for school supplies. He needs to buy
2 notebooks for $0.98 each. He also needs to buy
10 pencils for $0.20 each and 2 pens for $0.48 each.

9. Does he have enough money? How do you know?

_____

_____

_____

10. How much more or less than $5.00 do his school
supplies cost?

_____

▶ Look for "Easy" Combinations

You can sometimes find number combinations that make it
possible to add numbers mentally.

11. Add 243, 274, 252, and 231 vertically.

12. Explain how you can use number combinations to help
you add the numbers.

_____

_____

_____

Find the total. Add mentally if you can.

13.	14.	15.	16.	17.
8	46	35	348	147
4	21	29	516	182
6	+ 64	75	+ 492	108
+ 2		+ 61		+ 165

Estimation and Mental Math

▶ Understand a Take-Apart Situation

Jimmy dropped a 400-piece jigsaw puzzle and the pieces went all over his room. He found 264 of them. This is how he used his MathBoard to find out how many pieces were still missing.

Discuss each step of Jimmy's drawing.

1. Jimmy drew 400 and wrote the numbers for the problem.

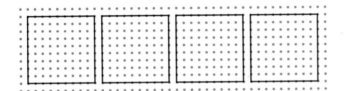

$$
\begin{array}{r}
400 \\
- \ 264 \\
\end{array}
$$

2. Jimmy saw that he had no tens and no ones. What do his drawing and the numbers show that he did next?

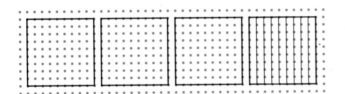

3. Then, what did he do to his drawing and numbers?

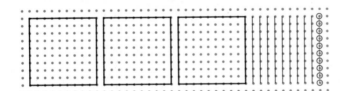

4. Next, he circled and drew a line through parts of the drawing. What does this show?

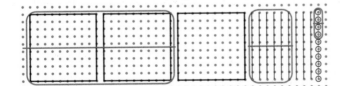

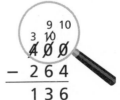

5. **On the Back** Explain how you ungroup 200 to subtract 25.

Subtract from Hundreds

Dear Family,

Your child is now learning about subtraction. A common subtraction mistake is subtracting in the wrong direction. Children may think that they always subtract the smaller digit from the larger digit, but this is not true. To help children avoid this mistake, the *Math Expressions* program encourages children to "fix" numbers first and then subtract.

$$\begin{array}{r} 6\cancel{3}4 \\ -\ \cancel{1}58 \\ \hline 5\cancel{2}4 \end{array}$$

When one or more digits in the top number are smaller than the corresponding digits in the bottom number, fix the numbers by "ungrouping." For example, 634 − 158 is shown below:

1. We cannot subtract 8 ones from 4 ones. We get more ones by ungrouping 1 ten to make 10 ones.

We now have 14 ones and only 2 tens.

$$\begin{array}{r} \overset{2\ \ 14}{6\,\cancel{3}\,\cancel{4}} \\ -\ 1\,5\,8 \\ \hline \end{array}$$

2. We cannot subtract 5 tens from 2 tens. We get more tens by ungrouping 1 hundred to make 10 tens.

We now have 12 tens and only 5 hundreds.

$$\begin{array}{r} \overset{12}{\underset{}{5\ \cancel{\overset{}{7}}\ 14}} \\ \cancel{6}\,\cancel{3}\,\cancel{4} \\ -\ 1\,5\,8 \\ \hline \end{array}$$

3. Now we can subtract:
5 − 1 = 4 hundreds
12 − 5 = 7 tens
14 − 8 = 6 ones

$$\begin{array}{r} \overset{12}{\underset{}{5\ \cancel{\overset{}{7}}\ 14}} \\ \cancel{6}\,\cancel{3}\,\cancel{4} \\ -\ 1\,5\,8 \\ \hline 4\,7\,6 \end{array}$$

In the method above, the numbers are ungrouped from right to left, but students can also ungroup from left to right. Children can choose whichever way works best for them. Once the ungrouping is completed, subtraction can also be performed either from right to left or from left to right.

Your child should also continue to practice multiplication and division skills at home.

If you have any questions or comments, please call or write me.

Sincerely,
Your child's teacher

Estimada familia:

Ahora su niño está aprendiendo a restar. Un error muy común al restar es hacerlo en la dirección equivocada. Los niños pueden pensar que siempre se le resta el dígito más pequeño del dígito más grande, pero no es verdad. Para ayudar a los niños a no cometer este error, el programa *Math Expressions* les propone "arreglar" los números primero y luego restar.

$$\begin{array}{r} 634 \\ -\ 158 \\ \hline 524 \end{array}$$

Cuando uno o más de los dígitos del número de arriba es más pequeño que el dígito correspondiente del número de abajo, se arreglan los números "desagrupándolos". Por ejemplo, 634 –158 se muestra abajo:

1. No podemos restar 8 unidades de 4 unidades. Obtenemos más unidades al desagrupar 1 decena para formar 10 unidades.

Ahora tenemos 14 unidades y solamente 2 decenas.

$$\begin{array}{r} {}^{2}\ 634^{14} \\ -\ 158 \end{array}$$

2. No podemos restar 5 decenas de 2 decenas. Obtenemos más decenas al desagrupar 1 centena para formar 10 decenas.

Ahora tenemos 12 decenas y solamente 5 centenas.

$$\begin{array}{r} {}^{12} \\ {}^{5}\ 634^{14} \\ -\ 158 \end{array}$$

3. Ahora podemos restar:

5 – 1 =
4 centenas
12 – 5 =
7 decenas
14 – 8 =
6 unidades

$$\begin{array}{r} {}^{12} \\ {}^{5}\ 634^{14} \\ -\ 158 \\ \hline 476 \end{array}$$

En el método de arriba se desagrupan los números de derecha a izquierda, pero también se pueden desagrupar de izquierda a derecha. Los niños pueden escoger la manera que les resulte más fácil. Una vez que hayan desagrupado, la resta también puede hacerse de derecha a izquierda o de izquierda a derecha.

Su niño también debe seguir practicando las destrezas de multiplicación y de división en casa.

Si tiene alguna pregunta o comentario, por favor comuníquese conmigo.

Atentamente,
El maestro de su niño

Subtract From Hundreds

Class Activity

Name _____

Date _____

Vocabulary

inverse operations
addend

► Draw and Solve Multi-Digit Addition

Addition and subtraction are **inverse operations**.
Break-apart drawings help to show inverse relationships.

1. Write a word problem that requires adding 257 and 143.

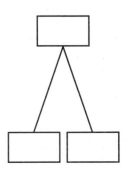

_____

_____

_____

_____

2. Write the **addends** in the break-apart drawing.

3. Discuss how this place-value drawing matches each
   addition method.

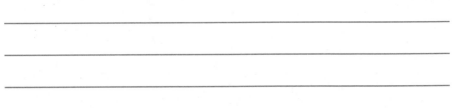

257

\+

143

10 ones = 1 new ten

9 tens + 1 new ten = 1 new hundred

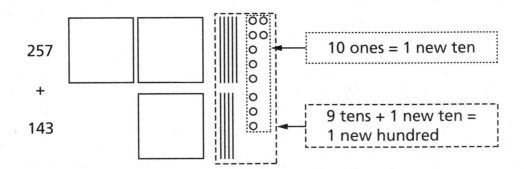

New Groups Above	New Groups Below	Show Subtotals
1 1		
257	257	257
+ 143	+ 143	+ 143
400	1 1	300
	400	90
		+ 10
		400

4. Complete the break-apart drawing next to problem 1.

Class Activity

▶ Draw and Solve Multi-Digit Subtraction

5. Write a word problem that requires subtracting 257 from 400.

_____

_____

_____

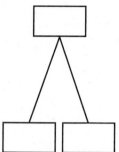

Discuss.

6. How does this drawing show ungrouping 1 hundred?

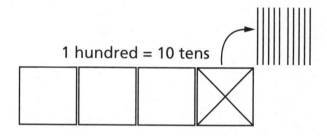

1 hundred = 10 tens

7. How does this drawing show ungrouping 1 ten?

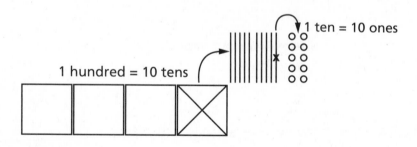

1 hundred = 10 tens   1 ten = 10 ones

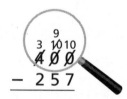

8. How does this drawing show the solution?

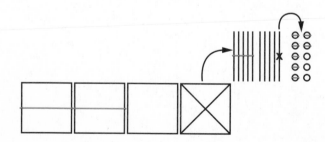

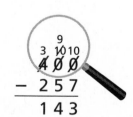

9. Explain how you ungroup 200 to subtract 25.

10. How can you use subtraction to check addition?

Subtraction Undoes Addition

Class Activity

▶ Ungroup Different Ways

Look at 864 − 586.

1. Which number does the drawing represent? _____

$$\begin{array}{r} 864 \\ - \ 586 \end{array}$$

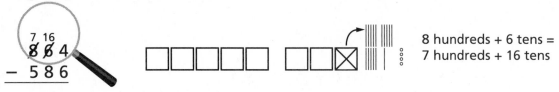

You can ungroup left-to-right as shown in problems 2 and 3 before you subtract.

2. Ungroup 1 hundred to see _____ more tens.

8 hundreds + 6 tens =
7 hundreds + 16 tens

3. Ungroup 1 ten to see _____ more ones.

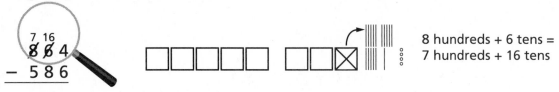

16 tens + 4 ones =
15 tens + 14 ones

You can ungroup right-to-left as shown in problems 4 and 5 before you subtract.

4. Ungroup 1 ten to see _____ more ones.

6 tens + 4 ones =
5 tens + 14 ones

5. Ungroup 1 hundred to see _____ more tens.

8 hundreds + 5 tens =
7 hundreds + 15 tens

Name _____

Date _____

▶ Subtraction and Money

You can use models to help you subtract money amounts.

Sondra had $140 to spend on new clothes for school. She bought a shirt for $21. To find out how much money she had left, use play money to act out the problem.

Sondra had _____ left.

Use play money to solve each problem.

Show your work.

1. Jason had $30. He gave $18 to his brother. How much money does Jason have left?

   _____

2. Elana's coach had $250 to spend on softball equipment. She spent $76 on bases. How much does the coach have left?

   _____

3. The school science club raised $325. After buying equipment for an experiment they had $168 left. How much did they spend?

   _____

4. Amy paid $575 for new furniture. Before buying it she had $813. How much did she have afterward?

   _____

5. Mrs. Washington has $265. She wants to buy shoes for $67 and dresses for $184. Does she have enough money? Explain your answer.

   _____

Ungroup for Any Subtraction

▶ Discuss Ungrouping With Zeros

Look inside the magnifying glass and discuss each ungrouping step.

1. Ungroup step-by-step: *or*   **2.** Ungroup all at once:

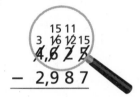

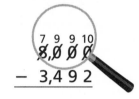

▶ Decide When to Ungroup

3. Ungroup left-to-right: *or*   **4.** Ungroup right-to-left:

▶ Other Ungrouping Situations

5. When we have zeros and other digits on the top:

6. When we have the same digit on the top and bottom:

7. On the Back Show how to subtract 4,238 from 5,003.

Subtract from Thousands

▶ Find and Correct Mistakes

Always check your work. Many mistakes can be easily fixed.

What is the mistake in each problem? How can you fix the mistake and find the correct answer?

1. 67,308 − 5,497

$$
\begin{array}{r}
6\ \overset{12}{\cancel{}}\overset{13}{\cancel{3}}\overset{10}{\cancel{}} \\
6\,7,\cancel{3}\,\cancel{0}\,8 \\
-5,4\,9\,7 \\
\hline
1\,2,3\,3\,8
\end{array}
$$

2. 134,865 − 5,294

$$
\begin{array}{r}
134,865 \\
-\ \ \ 5,294 \\
\hline
131,631
\end{array}
$$

_____   _____

_____   _____

_____   _____

_____   _____

_____   _____

▶ Check Subtraction by "Adding Up"

"Add up" to find any places where there is a subtraction mistake. Discuss how each mistake might have been made and correct the subtraction if necessary.

3. $\begin{array}{r} 163,406 \\ -\ \ 84,357 \\ \hline 79,159 \end{array}$ **4.** $\begin{array}{r} 526,741 \\ -\ 139,268 \\ \hline 413,473 \end{array}$ **5.** $\begin{array}{r} 2,380,043 \\ -\ \ 678,145 \\ \hline 1,701,908 \end{array}$ **6.** $\begin{array}{r} 5,472,639 \\ -\ 2,375,841 \\ \hline 3,096,798 \end{array}$

7. Write and solve a subtraction problem with numbers in the millions.

_____

_____

Name _____ **Date** _____

Going Further

▶ Estimate Differences

You can use estimation to decide if an answer is reasonable.

Dan did this subtraction: 8,196 − 5,980. His answer was 3,816. Discuss how using estimation can help you decide if his answer is correct.

Decide whether each answer is reasonable. Show your estimate.

1. 4,914 − 949 = 3,065

2. 52,022 − 29,571 = 22,451

_____

_____

_____

_____

Solve.

Show your work.

3. Bob has 3,226 marbles in his collection. Mia has 1,867 marbles. Bob says he has 2,359 more than Mia. Is Bob's answer reasonable? Show your estimate.

_____

4. Two towns have populations of 24,990 and 12,205. Gretchen says the difference is 12,785. Is Gretchen's answer reasonable? Show your estimate.

_____

5. Estimate to decide if the answer is reasonable. If it is not reasonable, describe the mistake and find the correct answer.

$$\begin{array}{r} 8,005,716 \\ -\ 2,900,905 \\ \hline 6,104,811 \end{array}$$

_____

_____

_____

Subtract Larger Numbers

▶ Use a Price List

School Supplies			
Pen	$0.19	Spiral notebook	$0.89
Pencil	$0.15	Loose-leaf paper (50 sheets)	$0.69
Colored markers (box of 8)	$1.49	Computer disk	$0.75
Pencil box	$0.70	Gym T-shirt	$3.50
Eraser	$0.15	Combination lock	$2.89

Answer each question. Explain your thinking.

Show your work.

1. Sylvia has $5.00 to buy a T-shirt. Will she have enough left to buy a box of markers?

   _____

   _____

2. Bo has $4.00. How many computer disks can he buy?

   _____

   _____

3. Bilana has $4.00. She wants to buy a combination lock, pencil box, and a notebook. Does she have enough?

   _____

   _____

   _____

4. Joseph has $2.00. He wants to buy a pack of paper and 2 erasers. Can he also buy 5 ball-point pens?

   _____

   _____

   _____

5. **Math Journal** Use the price list to write two word problems.

Name _____ **Date** _____

Vocabulary

acre

▶ **Use a Table With Larger Numbers**

This table shows the total area of some U.S. National Parks in **acres**. (1 acre = 4,840 square yards)

Park Name	State	Total Acres
Big Bend	Texas	801,163
Canyonlands	Utah	337,598
Carlsbad Caverns	New Mexico	46,766
Channel Islands	California	249,561
Everglades	Florida	1,508,538
Gates of the Arctic	Alaska	8,472,506
Glacier	Montana	1,013,572
Grand Canyon	Arizona	1,217,403
Great Smoky Mountains	North Carolina/Tennessee	521,752
Isle Royale	Michigan	571,790
Mammoth Cave	Kentucky	52,830
Olympic	Washington	922,651
Shenandoah	Virginia	199,045

Use the table to solve each problem.

Show your work.

6. Which is greater, the area of Big Bend National Park or the combined area of Channel Islands and Isle Royale parks? Estimate the difference and explain your thinking.

_____

_____

_____

_____

7. Which park is closest in area to the area of Canyonlands and Olympic parks combined?

_____

Estimate With Real-World Situations

► **Use a Table With Larger Numbers (continued)**

Show your work.

Use the table to solve each problem.

8. Estimate the total area of the three largest parks listed in the table. Show how you estimated.

_____

_____

9. What is the difference between the area of Great Smoky Mountains park and the area of Shenandoah park? Check your answer by rounding and estimating.

_____

10. Which park is about 4 times the area of Carlsbad Caverns park? Use estimation and explain your thinking.

_____

_____

_____

_____

► **Write Your Own Word Problems**

11. **Math Journal** Research some real-world data with large numbers. Make a table of the data. Then write two or three word problems using your data.

Going Further

Name _____ Date _____

Vocabulary

estimate

▶ Estimate or Exact Answer?

Decide whether you need an **estimate** or exact answer to solve each problem. Then solve the problem.

1. Miguel gave the clerk two $20 bills for a hat that cost $16.50 and a shirt that cost $12.00. How much change should Miguel receive?

_____

_____

2. Fairview Elementary has 564 students. Lincoln Elementary has 728 students. About how many students attend the two schools?

_____

_____

3. A school has a fundraising goal of selling 1,000 candles. They sell between 100 and 300 candles every day. How long will it take to meet their goal?

_____

_____

4. The Sanders family drove 421 miles to the beach. Coming home, they drove 366 miles to visit friends and then 207 miles home. About how many miles did they drive in all?

_____

_____

5. Sara wants a backpack that costs $38.95. She sees it on sale for $31.95 at a different store. How much cheaper is the backpack that is on sale?

_____

_____

▶ **Discuss Problem Types**

Think of a change, collection, or comparison problem for each exercise. Then write an equation to solve the problem.

1. $a + 278 = 747$

747
/ \
a   278

2. $b - 346 = 587$

b
/ \
346   587

3.

933
/ \
c   346

4.

747

| e | ⟨469⟩ |

▶ **Share Solutions**

Write an equation to solve each problem. Make a math drawing if you need to.

Show your work.

5. Of 800,000 species of insects, about 560,000 undergo complete metamorphosis. How many species do not undergo complete metamorphosis?

_____

_____

6. The Great Pyramid of Giza has about 2,000,000 stone blocks. A replica has 1,900,000 fewer blocks. How many blocks are in the replica?

_____

_____

7. Last year 439,508 people visited Fun World. This is 46,739 fewer visitors than this year. How many people visited Fun World this year?

_____

_____

▶ Share Solutions (continued)

8. At the end of a baseball game, there were 35,602 people in the stadium. There were 37,614 people there at the beginning of the game. How many people left before the game ended?

_____

_____

9. This year Pinnacle Publishing printed 64,924 more books than Premier Publishing. If Pinnacle printed 231,069 books, how many did Premier print?

_____

_____

10. Mary drove her car 2,483 miles during a road trip. Now she has 86,445 miles on her car. How many miles did her car have before her trip?

_____

_____

11. The Elbe River in Europe is 1,170 km long. The Yellow River in China is 5,465 km long. How long are the two rivers altogether?

_____

_____

12. A bridge is 1,595 feet long. Each cable holding up the bridge is 1,983 feet longer than the bridge itself. How long is each cable?

_____

_____

Write an equation, using a letter to represent the unknown. Then solve.

Show your work.

1. Gaddi exercised 30 minutes on the weekend. She exercised a total of 95 minutes for the week. How many minutes did she exercise on the weekdays?

_____

2. A trainer has 72 bottles of water to give away. By noon, he has 37 bottles of water. How many bottles of water did he give away before noon?

_____

Make a break-apart drawing. Then write and solve an equation, using a letter to represent the unknown.

3. In a collection of 128 marbles, 19 marbles are red. How many marbles in the collection are not red?

_____

Draw comparison bars. Write and solve an equation.

4. At the playground there are 5 slides. There are 7 more swings than slides. How many swings are there?

_____

Solve each problem mentally or use equations, comparison bars, or break-apart drawings.

5. Thomas is thinking of a number. If 8 is added to his number and 6 is subtracted from that sum, the result is 12. What is the number?

_____

6. Shana has a vase with 5 roses, 3 tulips, 14 carnations, and 23 daisies. How many more carnations than roses and tulips are in the vase?

Write the value of the underlined digit.

7. 59,<u>8</u>03 _____

8. 8,7<u>7</u>4,002 _____

Write each number in standard form.

9. seventy-five thousand, four hundred eight

_____

10. five million, sixty-nine thousand, seven hundred thirty-six

_____

Write >, <, or = to make each statement true.

11. 45,907 _____ 45,799

12. 728,925 _____ 729,825

Round to the nearest hundred.

13. 8,659 _____

Round to the nearest thousand.

14. 37,808 _____

Copy each exercise, lining up the places correctly. Then add or subtract.

15. 1,472 + 5,178 = _____

16. 25,097 + 57,336 = _____

17. 6,824 − 3,731 = _____

18. 57,875 − 43,088 = _____

19. 50,000 − 31,602 = _____

20. **Extended Response** Determine whether the following statement is true or false. Explain your thinking.

$$6,421 - (284 + 653) = (6,421 - 284) + 653$$

_____

_____

▶ Define One-Dimensional Figures

Write the name of each figure.

1.

_____

2.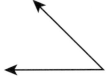

_____

3.

_____

4.

_____

5.

_____

6.

_____

7.

_____

8.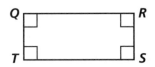

_____

9. What is the name of this figure? Use the letters to name each of its **angles**.

_____

10. A rectangle has four right angles. How can you remember that rectangles have right angles?

_____

_____

11. Draw and label a line, a line segment, a ray, and an angle.

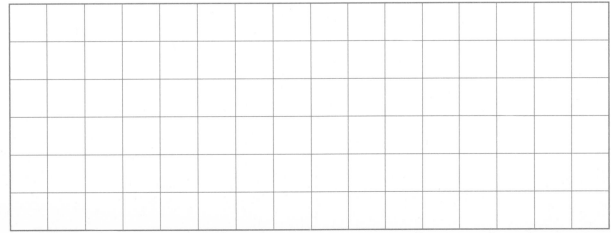

► **Discuss Angles**

Angles can be many different sizes.

Discuss the groups of angles.

12. How are all these acute angles alike?

_____

_____

13. How is an acute angle different from a right angle?

_____

_____

14. How are all of these obtuse angles alike?

_____

_____

15. How are they different from a right angle?

_____

_____

16. How are they different from an acute angle?

_____

_____

▶ Classify Angles

**Name each angle using the letters. Label each angle as
right, acute, or obtuse.**

17.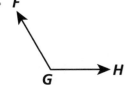

_____

_____

18.

_____

_____

19.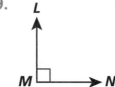

_____

_____

20. Use letters to name two acute and two obtuse angles in
this figure. Label each as obtuse or acute.

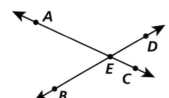

_____

_____

_____

_____

21. Draw and label a right angle, an acute angle, and
an obtuse angle.

▶ Angles in the Real World

Here is a map of Jon's neighborhood. The east and west
streets are named for presidents of the United States. The
north and south streets are numbered. The avenues have
letters. Jon's house is on the corner of Lincoln and First.

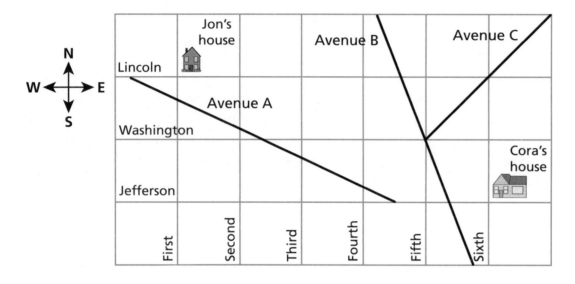

22. What do the arrows to the left of the map tell you?

_____

23. Jon leaves his house and rides his bike south on First.
    What kind of angle does he make for each turn in this
    route?

    • He turns southeast onto avenue A. _____

    • When he reaches Washington, he turns west. _____

    • When he gets back to First, he turns south. _____

24. Jon's cousin Cora rides east on Lincoln from Jon's house
    to avenue C. What kind of angle will she make if she
    turns northeast? if she turns southwest?

_____

Name Angles

▶ More Angles in the Real World

Look at the map of Jon's neighborhood on page 184.

25. Cora lives at the corner of Jefferson and Sixth. Record three different routes she can use to get from her house to Jon's house. For each route, tell what kind of angle each turn makes.

_____

_____

_____

_____

_____

_____

_____

_____

_____

_____

26. Write what you know about right, acute, and obtuse angles.

_____

_____

_____

_____

_____

_____

_____

_____

_____

_____

Going Further

Vocabulary

translation

▶ Translate Figures

A **translation** is also called a slide. Translate vertex *A* to point *B*. Copy each figure at the new location.

1.

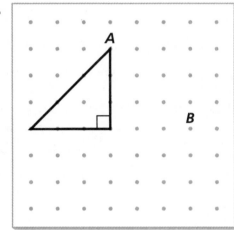

2.

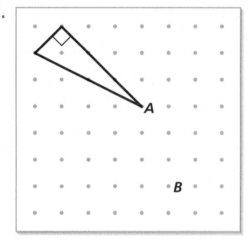

3.

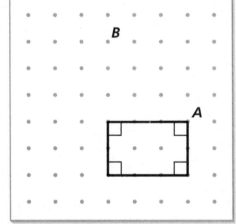

4.

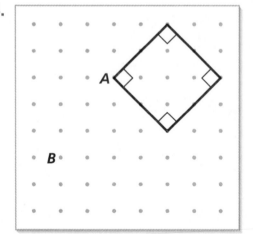

5. Explain the difference between a reflection and a translation. Use the letter P in your explanation.

_____

_____

_____

_____

Name Angles

Dear Family,

This unit is your child's second short geometry unit. It is about the different kinds of triangles.

Right
triangle

One right
angle (90°)

Acute
triangle

All angles
less than 90°

Obtuse
triangle

One angle
greater than 90°

Equilateral
triangle

All three sides
congruent
(equal size)

Isosceles
triangle

Two sides
congruent

Scalene
triangle

Three different
sides

Your child will also discover the standard method for finding the perimeter of a triangle (side + side + side) and the area of a triangle ($\frac{1}{2}$ × base × height).

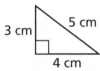

3 cm 5 cm

4 cm

Perimeter (*P*) = 3 cm + 4 cm + 5 cm = 12 cm

Area (*A*) = $\frac{1}{2}$ × 4 cm × 3 cm = 6 square cm

Be sure that your child continues to review and practice the basics of multiplication and division. A good understanding of the basics will be very important later in the year when students learn more difficult concepts in multiplication and division.

If you have any questions or comments, please call or write to me.

Thank you.

Sincerely,
Your child's teacher

Estimada familia:

Ésta es la segunda unidad corta de geometría que ve su niño. Presenta diferentes tipos de triángulos.

Triángulo rectángulo

Tiene un ángulo recto (90°)

Triángulo acutángulo

Todos los ángulos son menores de 90°

Triángulo obtusángulo

Tiene un ángulo mayor de 90°

Triángulo equilátero

Los tres lados son congruentes (mismo tamaño)

Triángulo isósceles

Dos lados son congruentes

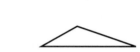

Triángulo escaleno

Los tres lados son diferentes

Su niño también aprenderá el método normal para hallar el perímetro de un triángulo (lado + lado + lado) y el área de un triángulo ($\frac{1}{2}$ × base × altura).

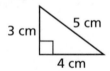

Perímetro (P) = 3 cm + 4 cm + 5 cm = 12 cm

Área (A) = $\frac{1}{2}$ × 4 cm × 3 cm = 6 cm cuadrados

Asegúrese de que su niño siga repasando y practicando las multiplicaciones y divisiones básicas. Es importante que comprenda las operaciones básicas para que pueda aprender conceptos de multiplicación y división más difíciles.

Si tiene alguna pregunta o comentario, por favor comuníquese conmigo.

Gracias.

Atentamente,
El maestro de su niño

Name Angles

Vocabulary
right triangle
obtuse triangle
acute triangle

▶ **Discuss Angles of a Triangle**

The prefix *tri-* means "three," so it is easy to remember that a triangle has 3 angles. Triangles can take their names from the kind of angles they have.

- A **right triangle** has one right angle, which we show by drawing a small square at the right angle.

- An **obtuse triangle** has one obtuse angle.

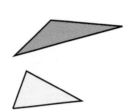

- An **acute triangle** has three acute angles.

1. You can also use letters to write and talk about triangles. This triangle is △QRS. Name its three angles and their type.

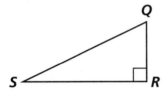

_____

_____

_____

2. What kind of triangle is △QRS? How do you know?

_____

_____

3. Draw and label a right triangle, an acute triangle, and an obtuse triangle.

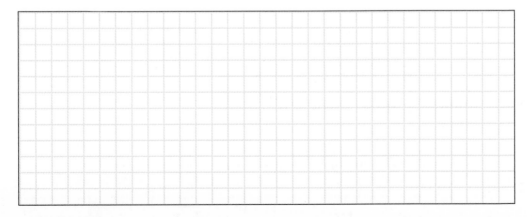

▶ Identify Angles of a Triangle

Name each triangle by its angles. Explain your thinking.

4.

_____

_____

5.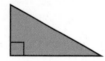

_____

_____

6.

_____

_____

7.

_____

_____

8.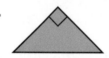

_____

_____

9.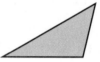

_____

_____

10.

_____

_____

11.

_____

_____

12.

_____

_____

13.

_____

_____

14.

_____

_____

15.

_____

_____

16. Describe how angles make triangles different from one another.

_____

_____

Class Activity

► Discuss Sides of a Triangle

Vocabulary

congruent
equilateral
isosceles
scalene

Triangles can be named for their sides. Small perpendicular marks on the sides of triangles tell us when sides are **congruent**.

• The prefix *equi-* means "equal." Triangles that have three congruent sides are called **equilateral**.

• Triangles that have two congruent sides are called **isosceles**. The word *isosceles* comes from very old words that mean "equal legs."

• Triangles with no congruent sides are called **scalene**. All triangles that are not equilateral or isosceles are scalene.

Use these triangles to answer the questions.

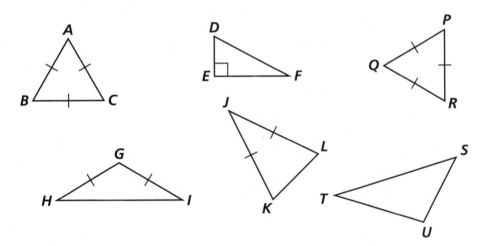

17. Write the letter names of the scalene triangles.

_____

18. Write the letter names of the equilateral triangles.

_____

19. Write the letter names of the isosceles triangles.

_____

Class Activity

▶ Identify Sides of a Triangle

Name each triangle by its sides. Explain your thinking.

20.

_____

_____

21.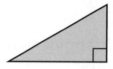

_____

_____

22.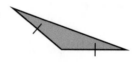

_____

_____

23.

_____

_____

24.

_____

_____

25.

_____

_____

26.

_____

_____

27.

_____

_____

28.

_____

_____

29.

_____

_____

30.

_____

_____

31.

_____

_____

32. Explain how sides make triangles different from each other.

_____

_____

▶ Possible Ways to Name Triangles

33. Can triangles be named for both their sides and their angles? Explain your thinking.

_____

_____

Draw each triangle. If you can't, explain why.

34. Draw a right scalene triangle.	**35.** Draw an obtuse scalene triangle.
36. Draw a right equilateral triangle.	**37.** Draw an acute isosceles triangle.
38. Draw an obtuse equilateral triangle.	**39.** Draw a right isosceles triangle.

Going Further

► Sort Triangles in Different Ways

Write a capital letter and a lowercase letter inside each triangle using the keys to the right.

Cut out the triangles and use the Venn diagram to sort them in different ways.

| acute = a |
| obtuse = o |
| right = r |

| Isosceles = I |
| Scalene = S |
| Equilateral = E |

Triangles

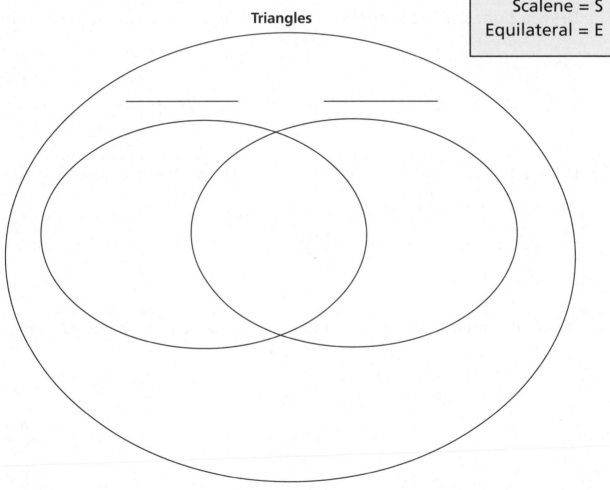

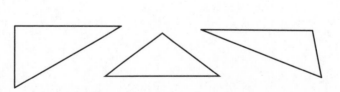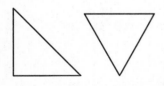

Name Triangles

Class Activity

Vocabulary

quadrilateral
congruent

▶ Build Quadrilaterals With Triangles

You can make a **quadrilateral** by joining two **congruent** triangles together along corresponding sides.

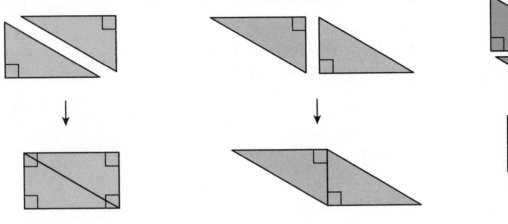 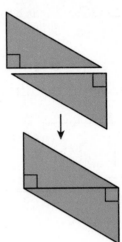

Cut out the congruent triangles below. For each exercise, glue two of the triangles to the paper so that the stated sides are joined. Then write the name of the quadrilateral.

1. *AB* is joined to *AB*   **2.** *AC* is joined to *AC*   **3.** *BC* is joined to *BC*

_____   _____   _____

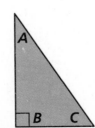 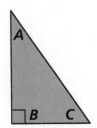 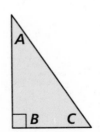 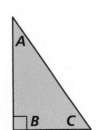 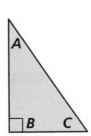 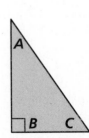

▶ Match Quadrilaterals With Triangles

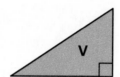 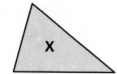

Name the triangle that is used twice to form each of the following quadrilaterals. Then name the quadrilateral.

4.
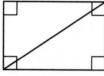

_____

_____

5.
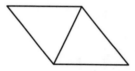

_____

_____

6.

_____

_____

7.

_____

_____

8.
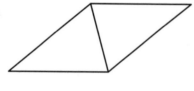

_____

_____

9.
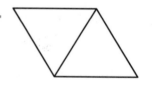

_____

_____

Name _____   **Date** _____

▶ **Make Triangles With Diagonals**

A **diagonal** connects opposite angles of a quadrilateral. You can make triangles by drawing a diagonal on a quadrilateral.

Name each quadrilateral. Then use letters to name the triangles you can make with the diagonals.

10.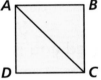

_____   _____   _____

11.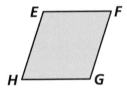

_____   _____   _____

12.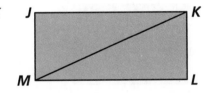

_____   _____   _____

13.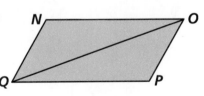

_____   _____   _____

Going Further

Name _____ **Date** _____

► Identify Rotated Figures

1. Name each triangle by its angles and by its sides.

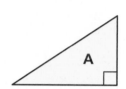 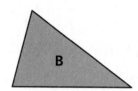 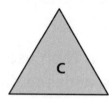 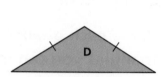

_____ _____ _____ _____

2. Each triangle above has been rotated and is shown below. Label each triangle with the correct letter.

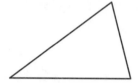 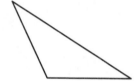 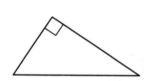

_____ _____ _____ _____

Label the vertices of the rotated quadrilaterals.

3.

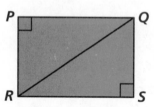 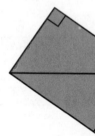

4.

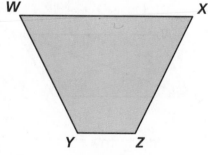 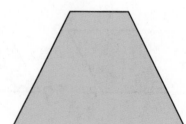

Triangles and Diagonals

Vocabulary

perimeter

▶ Find the Perimeter of Triangles

Think about what you already know about finding perimeter. Discuss a method that will work to find the perimeter of each quadrilateral.

1.
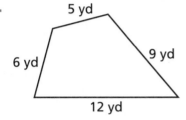

_____

2.
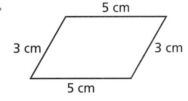

_____

3.
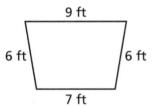

_____

4.
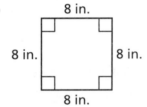

_____

5. Which method will work for any quadrilateral?

_____

6. Will a similar method work to find the perimeter of any triangle? Why?

_____

_____

Tell what other methods will work with each of these triangles. Solve.

7.
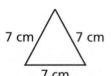

_____

8.
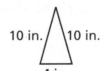

_____

9.
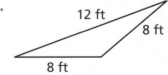

_____

Class Activity

Name

Date

▶ Find the Area of Right Triangles

10. Draw a congruent triangle along the side marked *d* and write the name of the quadrilateral this makes.

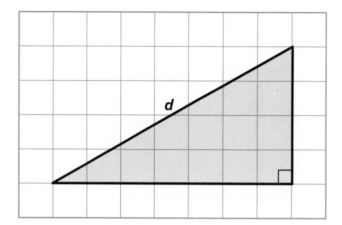

_____

11. What is the **area** of the quadrilateral?
What is half of that number?

_____

_____

12. What figure is half of the quadrilateral?
What is the area of that figure?

_____

_____

13. Which triangle measurement did you not use? Why?

_____

_____

14. Write a formula to find the area of a right triangle.

_____

_____

▶ Find the Area of Other Triangles

15. Draw a congruent triangle along the side marked *d*.
Write the name of the quadrilateral this makes.

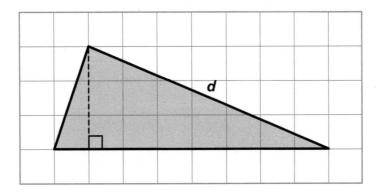

_____

16. What measurement does the dotted line represent
in the triangle above?

_____

17. Why do you need the height to find the area of the
quadrilateral?

_____

_____

18. Why do you also need the height to find the area of
the triangle?

_____

_____

_____

19. Write a formula to find the area of any triangle.

_____

_____

Class Activity

▶ Find Perimeter and Area of Triangles

Use your centimeter ruler to measure each triangle.
Then find its perimeter and area.

20.

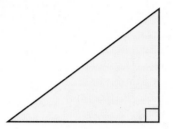

_____

_____

_____

21.

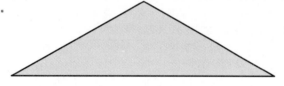

_____

_____

_____

22.

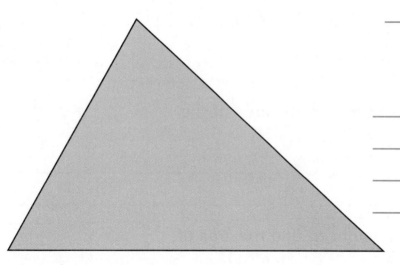

_____

_____

_____

_____

23.

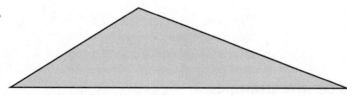

_____

_____

_____

_____

Name each triangle by its angles. Explain your thinking.

1.

_____

2.

_____

3.

_____

Use these triangles to answer questions 4–6.

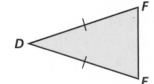
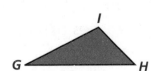

4. Write the letter name of the scalene triangle.

_____

5. Write the letter name of the equilateral triangle.

_____

6. Draw a diagonal. Describe the triangles formed.

_____

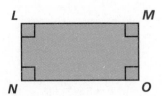

Find the perimeter and area of each triangle.

7.

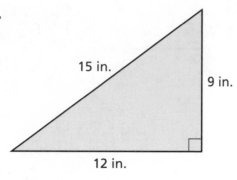

15 in.

9 in.

12 in.

Perimeter _____

Area _____

8.

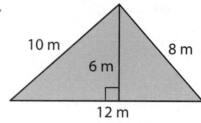

10 m

6 m

8 m

12 m

Perimeter _____

Area _____

Use the following information to solve problems 9 and 10.

Farida made a pennant for her school in the shape of a right triangle. It has a base of 12 in. and a height of 5 in. Its other side is 13 in. long.

9. Farida placed a ribbon border along the edges of the pennant. How many inches of ribbon did she need?

_____

Show your work.

10. **Extended Response** Farida made the pennant by cutting up a 10-inch square cloth and sewing the pieces together. How many square inches of cloth did Farida have left over? Explain your thinking.

_____

_____

_____

Class Activity

Vocabulary

array
area

▶ Model a Product of Ones

The number of unit squares in an **array** of connected unit squares is the **area** of the rectangle formed by the squares. We sometimes just show the measurement of length and width.

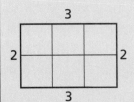

You can draw a rectangle for any multiplication. In the real world, we use multiplication for finding both sizes of arrays and areas of figures.

A 2 × 3 rectangle has 6 unit squares inside, so 2 × 3 = 6.

1. On your MathBoard, draw a 3 × 2 rectangle. How is the 3 × 2 rectangle similar to the 2 × 3 rectangle? How is it different?

_____

_____

_____

_____

2. How do the areas of the 2 × 3 and 3 × 2 rectangles compare?

_____

_____

▶ Factor the Tens to Multiply Ones and Tens

This 2 × 30 rectangle contains 6 groups of 10 square units, so its area is 60 square units.

```
30 =      10        +        10        +        10
  1 │  1 × 10 = 10  │  1 × 10 = 10   │  1 × 10 = 10  │ 1
  1 │  1 × 10 = 10  │  1 × 10 = 10   │  1 × 10 = 10  │ 1
          10        +        10        +        10
```

3. How can we show this numerically? Complete the steps.

   $2 \times 30 = (2 \times 1) \times (\underline{\hspace{1cm}} \times 10)$

   $= (\underline{\hspace{1cm}} \times \underline{\hspace{1cm}}) \times (1 \times 10)$

   $= \underline{\hspace{1cm}} \times 10 = 60$

4. On your MathBoard, draw a 30 × 2 rectangle and find its area.

   _____

5. How is the 30 × 2 rectangle similar to the 2 × 30 rectangle? How is it different?

   _____

   _____

   _____

   _____

6. Write out the steps for finding 4 × 20 by factoring the tens. Use your MathBoard if you need to.

   _____

   _____

   _____

▶ Model a Product of Tens

7. Find the area of this 20 × 30 rectangle by dividing it into 10-by-10 squares of 100.

▶ Factor the Tens

8. Complete the steps to show your work in problem 7 numerically.

$$20 \times 30 = (\underline{\hspace{1cm}} \times 10) \times (\underline{\hspace{1cm}} \times 10)$$

$$= (\underline{\hspace{1cm}} \times \underline{\hspace{1cm}}) \times (10 \times 10)$$

$$= \underline{\hspace{1cm}} \times 100$$

$$= 600$$

9. Is it true that 20 × 30 = 30 × 20? Explain how you know.

_____

10. Write out the steps for finding 40 × 20 by factoring the tens. Use your MathBoard if you need to.

_____

_____

Class Activity

▶ **Compare Equations**

In this lesson, you looked at these three equations.

$2 \times 3 = 6$ $2 \times 30 = 60$ $20 \times 30 = 600$

11. How are the three equations similar?

_____

_____

_____

12. How are the three equations different?

_____

_____

_____

13. How is the number of zeros in the factors related to the number of zeros in the product?

_____

_____

_____

Multiplication Arrays

Dear Family,

In this unit, your child will be learning about the common multiplication method that most adults know. However, they will also explore ways to draw multiplication. *Math Expressions* uses area of rectangles to show multiplication.

	30	+	7
20	$20 \times 30 = 600$		$20 \times 7 = 140$
+			
4	$4 \times 30 = 120$		$4 \times 7 = 28$

Area Method:

$20 \times 30 = 600$
$20 \times 7 = 140$
$4 \times 30 = 120$
$\underline{4 \times 7 = 28}$
Total = 888

Shortcut Method:

$\overset{1}{\underset{2}{}}$
37
$\underline{\times 24}$
148
$\underline{74}$
888

Area drawings help all students see multiplication. They also help students remember what numbers they need to multiply and what numbers make up the total.

Your child will also learn to find products involving single-digit numbers, tens, and hundreds by factoring the tens or hundreds. For example,

$$200 \times 30 = 2 \times 100 \times 3 \times 10$$
$$= 2 \times 3 \times 100 \times 10$$
$$= 6 \times 1{,}000 = 6{,}000$$

By observing the zeros patterns in products like these, your child will learn to do such multiplications mentally.

If your child is still not confident with single-digit multiplication and division, we urge you to set aside a few minutes every night for multiplication and division practice. In a few more weeks, the class will be doing multi-digit division, so it is very important that your child be both fast and accurate with basic multiplication and division.

If you need practice materials, please contact your child's teacher.

Sincerely,
Your child's teacher

Estimada familia:

En esta unidad, su niño estará aprendiendo el método de multiplicación común que la mayoría de los adultos conoce. Sin embargo, también explorará maneras de dibujar la multiplicación. Para mostrar la multiplicación, *Math Expressions* usa el método del área del rectángulo.

	30	+	7
20	20 × 30 = 600		20 × 7 = 140
+			
4	4 × 30 = 120		4 × 7 = 28

Método del área

20 × 30 = 600
20 × 7 = 140
4 × 30 = 120
4 × 7 = 28
Total = 888

Método más corto

$\frac{1}{2}$
37
× 24
148
74
888

Los dibujos de área ayudan a todos los estudiantes a visualizar la multiplicación. También ayudan a que los estudiantes recuerden qué números tienen que multiplicar y qué números forman el total.

Su niño también aprenderá a hallar productos a partir de números de un solo dígito, decenas y centenas factorizando las decenas o las centenas. Por ejemplo:

200 × 30 = 2 × 100 × 3 × 10
= 2 × 3 × 100 × 10
= 6 × 1,000 = 6,000

Al observar los patrones de ceros en productos como éstos, su niño aprenderá a hacer dichas multiplicaciones mentalmente.

Si su niño todavía no domina la multiplicación y la división con números de un solo dígito, le rogamos que le dedique algunos minutos todas las noches para practicar la multiplicación y la división. Dentro de pocas semanas, la clase hará divisiones con números de varios dígitos, por eso es muy importante que su niño haga las operaciones básicas de multiplicación y de división de manera rápida y exacta.

Si necesita materiales para practicar, comuníquese conmigo.

Atentamente,
El maestro de su niño

Multiplication Arrays

Class Activity

► Look for Patterns

Multiplying large numbers in your head is easier when you learn patterns of multiplication with tens.

Start with column A and look for the patterns used to get the expressions in each column. Complete the table.

Table 1

	A	B	C	D
	2 × 3	2 × 1 × 3 × 1	6 × 1	6
1.	2 × 30	2 × 1 × 3 × 10	6 × 10	_____
2.	20 × 30	2 × 10 × 3 × 10	_____	_____

3. How are the expressions in column B different from the expressions in column A?

_____

_____

_____

4. In column C, we see that each expression can be written as a number times a place value. Which of these **factors** gives more information about the size of the **product**?

_____

5. Why is 6 the first digit of the products in column D?

_____

6. Why are there different numbers of zeros in the products in column D?

_____

_____

Name _____   Date _____

▶ **Compare Tables**

Complete each table.

Table 2

	A	B	C	D
	6 × 3	6 × 1 × 3 × 1	18 × 1	18
7.	6 × 30	6 × 1 × 3 × 10	18 × 10	____
8.	60 × 30	6 × 10 × 3 × 10	____	____

Table 3

	A	B	C	D
	5 × 8	5 × 1 × 8 × 1	40 × 1	40
9.	5 × 80	5 × 1 × 8 × 10	40 × 10	____
10.	50 × 80	____	____	____

11. Why do the products in Table 2 have more digits than the products in Table 1?

_____

_____

12. Why are there more zeros in the products in Table 3 than those in Table 2?

_____

_____

Mental Math and Multiplication with Tens

Class Activity

Vocabulary

area
square units

▶ Explore the Area Model

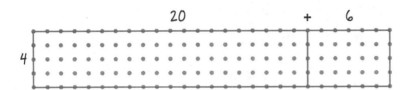

1. How many **square units** of **area** are there in the tens part of the drawing? _____

2. What multiplication equation gives the area of the tens part of the drawing? _____ Write this equation in its rectangle.

3. How many square units of area are there in the ones part? _____

4. What multiplication equation gives the area of the ones part? _____ Write this equation in its rectangle.

5. What is the total of the two areas? _____

6. How do you know that 104 is the correct product of 4 × 26?

_____

7. Read problems A and B.

   A. Al's photo album has 26 pages. Each page has 4 photos. How many photos are in Al's album?

   B. Nick took 4 photos. Henri took 26 photos. How many more photos did Henri take than Nick?

   Which problem could you solve using the multiplication you just did? Explain why.

_____

_____

_____

Class Activity

▶ Use Rectangles to Multiply

**Draw a rectangle for each problem on your MathBoard.
Find the tens product, the ones product, and the total.**

8. 3 × 28

9. 3 × 29

10. 5 × 30

11. 5 × 36

_____

_____

_____

12. 4 × 38

13. 8 × 38

14. 4 × 28

15. 5 × 28

_____

_____

_____

Solve each problem.

Show your work.

16. Maria's father planted 12 rows of tomatoes in his garden. Each row had 6 plants. How many tomato plants were in Maria's father's garden?

_____

17. The bakery can ice their cakes with chocolate, strawberry, or vanilla icing. The bakery has a total of 67 different ways to decorate iced cakes. How many different combinations of icing and decorations can the bakery make?

_____

18. Complete this word problem. Then solve it.

_____ has _____ boxes of _____.

There are _____ _____ in each box.

How many _____ does _____

have altogether? _____

Model One-Digit by Two-Digit Multiplication

Going Further

▶ Multiply One-Digit Dollar Amounts by Two-Digit Numbers

You can use your skills for multiplying a one-digit number by a two-digit number to multiply one-digit dollar amounts by two-digit numbers.

Find the exact cost. Give your answer in dollars.

Show your work.

1. A package of paper costs $2. If someone is purchasing 24 packages, how much will it cost?

_____

2. A box lunch can be purchased for $3. How much will 83 lunches cost?

_____

3. A movie ticket costs $8 per person. If 61 people go to the five o'clock show, how much money does the theater make for that show?

_____

4. A round-trip train ticket is $4 per person. If 58 fourth-graders take a field trip to the city on the train, how much will the train tickets cost?

_____

5. The admission to the zoo is $5 per person. If a group of 72 students takes a field trip to the zoo, how much will their tickets cost altogether?

_____

6. Sara earns $9 per hour as a cashier. How much does she earn in a 40-hour week?

_____

Going Further

▶ Multiply Two-Digit Dollar Amounts by One-Digit Numbers

You can use your skills for multiplying a one-digit number by a two-digit number to multiply one-digit numbers by two-digit dollar amounts.

Find the exact cost. Give your answer in dollars.

Show your work.

7. A bike costs $53. If 2 bikes are purchased, how much will be the total cost?

_____

8. A store sells CDs for $14. If someone buys 7 of them, how much will they cost altogether?

_____

9. An amusement park entrance fee is $23 per person. If 4 friends go to the amusement park, how much will their tickets cost altogether?

_____

10. A hotel costs $72 per night. How much will it cost to stay 3 nights?

_____

11. An airplane ticket costs $87. How much will 6 tickets cost?

_____

12. Jorge earns $99 each week. He goes on vacation in 9 weeks. How much will he earn before his vacation?

_____

Name _____ Date _____

Vocabulary

estimate
rounding

▶ **Estimate Products**

It is easier to **estimate** the product of a two-digit number and a one-digit number when you think about the two multiples of ten close to the two-digit number. This is shown in the drawings below.

1. In each drawing, find the rectangles that represent 4 × 70 and 4 × 60. These rectangles "frame" the rectangles for 4 × 63 and 4 × 68. Find the values of 4 × 70 and 4 × 60.

   4 × 70 = _____   4 × 60 = _____

2. Look at the rectangle that represents 4 × 68. Is 4 × 68 closer to 4 × 60 or to 4 × 70? So is 4 × 68 closer to 240 or 280?

   _____

3. Look at the rectangle that represents 4 × 63. Is 4 × 63 closer to 4 × 60 or to 4 × 70? Is 4 × 63 closer to 240 or 280?

   _____

4. Explain how to use **rounding** to estimate the product of a one-digit number and a two-digit number.

   _____

   _____

   _____

   _____

▶ Practice Estimation

Discuss how rounding and estimation could help solve these problems.

5. Keesha's school has 185 fourth-grade students. The library has 28 tables with 6 chairs at each table. Can all of the fourth-graders sit in the library at one time? How do you know?

_____

_____

_____

_____

6. Ameena is printing the class newsletter. There are 8 pages in the newsletter, and she needs 74 copies. Each package of paper contains 90 sheets. How many packages of paper does she need to print the newsletter?

_____

_____

_____

_____

Estimate each product. Then solve to check your estimate.

7. 3 × 52 _____

8. 7 × 48 _____

9. 9 × 27 _____

10. 8 × 34 _____

11. 8 × 35 _____

12. 5 × 22 _____

Estimate Products

▶ Numeric Multiplication Methods

You have used the area model to help you multiply.
In this lesson, you will learn some numeric multiplication
methods that are related to this area model.

Expanded Notation Method

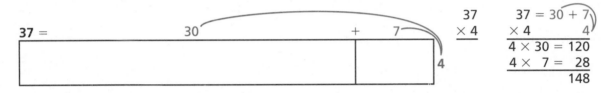

$$37 = 30 + 7$$
$$\times 4 \qquad\qquad 4$$
$$4 \times 30 = 120$$
$$4 \times 7 = \underline{\ 28}$$
$$148$$

Algebraic Notation Method

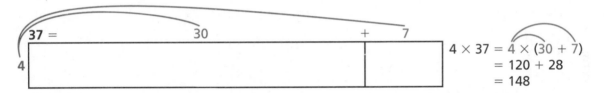

$$4 \times 37 = 4 \times (30 + 7)$$
$$= 120 + 28$$
$$= 148$$

▶ Connect the Multiplication Methods

Refer to the examples above.

1. What two values are added together to give the answer
   in the Expanded Notation Method?

   _____

2. What two values are added together to give the answer
   in the Algebraic Notation Method?

   _____

3. Choose one of the numeric methods and explain how it
   relates to the Rectangle Sections Method.

   _____

   _____

   _____

   _____

► Practice Multiplication

Fill in the blanks in the following solutions.

4. 4 × 86

Expanded Notation

$$86 = \underline{\hspace{1cm}} + 6$$
$$\times \quad 4 = \qquad \underline{\hspace{1cm}}$$
_____
$$4 \times \underline{\hspace{1cm}} = \underline{\hspace{1cm}}$$
$$\underline{\hspace{1cm}} \times 6 = \quad 24$$
_____

$$\underline{\hspace{1cm}}$$

Algebraic Notation

$$4 \cdot 86 = \underline{\hspace{1cm}} \cdot (80 + 6)$$
$$= 320 + \underline{\hspace{1cm}}$$
$$= \underline{\hspace{1cm}}$$

5. 4 × 68

Expanded Notation

$$\underline{\hspace{1cm}} = 60 + 8$$
$$\times \quad 4 = \qquad \underline{\hspace{1cm}}$$
_____
$$4 \times \underline{\hspace{1cm}} = \underline{\hspace{1cm}}$$
$$\underline{\hspace{1cm}} \times 8 = \quad 32$$
_____

$$\underline{\hspace{1cm}}$$

Algebraic Notation

$$4 \cdot 68 = 4 \cdot (\underline{\hspace{1cm}} + \underline{\hspace{1cm}})$$
$$= 240 + \underline{\hspace{1cm}}$$
$$= \underline{\hspace{1cm}}$$

Solve using a numeric method. Sketch a rectangle if necessary.

6. 5 × 64 = _____

7. 6 × 72 = _____

8. 7 × 92 = _____

9. 8 × 53 = _____

10. 5 × 46 = _____

11. 6 × 27 = _____

► Compare Multiplication Methods

Compare these methods for solving 9 × 28.

Method A	Method B	Method C	Method D	Method E
28 = 20 + 8	28 = 20 + 8	28	28	$\overset{7}{28}$
× 9 = 9	× 9 = 9	× 9	× 9	× 9
9 × 20 = 180	180	180	72	252
9 × 8 = 72	72	72	180	
252	252	252	252	

1. How are all the methods similar? List at least two similarities.

_____

_____

_____

2. How are the methods different? List at least three differences.

_____

_____

_____

► Analyze the Shortcut Method

Method E can be broken down into 2 steps.

Method E:	Step 1	Step 2
	$\overset{7}{28}$	$\overset{7}{28}$
	× 9	× 9
	2	252

3. Where are the products 180 and 72 from methods A–D?

_____

_____

_____

Class Activity

Name _____ Date _____

▶ Practice Multiplication

Solve using any method. Sketch a rectangle if necessary.
Check your answer by rounding and estimating.

4. 5 × 63 = _____

5. 39 × 8 = _____

6. 98 × 2 = _____

7. 4 × 86 = _____

8. 7 × 25 = _____

9. 47 × 9 = _____

10. 3 × 72 = _____

11. 6 × 54 = _____

Discuss Different Methods

Going Further

Vocabulary
double bar graph

▶ Use Double Bar Graphs

The owner of a bike store wants to know how many of each type of bike she sells. She makes a **double bar graph** that shows the sales of each type for the last three years.

Bike Sales

Number Sold / Year

Mountain Bikes
Road Bikes

Answer each question using the double bar graph.

Show your work.

1. In which year were the most mountain bikes sold? How many were sold that year?

   _____

2. In which year were the most road bikes sold? How many were sold that year?

   _____

3. In which year were the fewest bikes sold? How many bikes were sold that year?

   _____

4. In 2002, how many more road bikes were sold than mountain bikes?

   _____

5. In 2004, how many more mountain bikes were sold than road bikes?

   _____

6. **On the Back** Make a double bar graph of some characteristic about boys and girls in your class, such as eye color or favorite sport.

Discuss Different Methods

Class Activity

3–7

Name _____ **Date** _____

▶ Compare the Three Methods

You can use the **Rectangle Sections Method** to multiply a
one-digit number by a three-digit number.

237 =	200	+	30	+	7	
4	4 × 200 = 800		4 × 30 = 120		4 × 7 = 28	4

$$\begin{aligned} 800 \\ 120 \\ +\ \ 28 \\ \hline 948 \end{aligned}$$

1. What are the two steps used to find the product of
   4 × 237 using the Rectangle Sections Method.

_____

The **Expanded Notation Method** uses the same steps as the
Rectangle Sections Method.

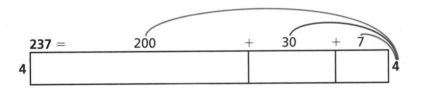

237 =	200	+	30	+	7	
4						4

$$\begin{aligned}
237 &= 200 + 30 + 7 \\
\times 4 & \qquad\qquad\qquad 4 \\
\hline
4 \times 200 &= 800 \\
4 \times 30 &= 120 \\
4 \times 7 &= \ \ 28 \\
\hline
& \ \ 948
\end{aligned}$$

2. What is the last step in the Expanded Notation Method
   and the Rectangle Sections Method?

_____

The **Algebraic Notation Method** uses expanded notation
just like the other two methods. Even though the steps look
different, they are the same as in the other methods.

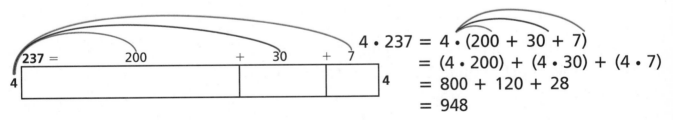

237 =	200	+	30	+	7	
4						4

$$\begin{aligned}
4 \cdot 237 &= 4 \cdot (200 + 30 + 7) \\
&= (4 \cdot 200) + (4 \cdot 30) + (4 \cdot 7) \\
&= 800 + 120 + 28 \\
&= 948
\end{aligned}$$

3. What is the first step in all three methods?

_____

Going Further

▶ Problem Solving with Money

You can use methods for multiplying a one-digit number by a three-digit number to multiply a money amount by a whole number.

Find the exact cost. Give your answer in cents and then give it in dollars.

Show your work.

1. A one-hour paddleboat rental costs $9.95. How much would it cost to rent 6 paddleboats for an hour?

   _____

2. A salad bar costs $8.25. How much would it cost for a family of four to eat at the salad bar?

   _____

3. A can of cat food costs $0.79. How much do 9 cans cost?

   _____

4. A club is making tie-dyed T-shirts from white T-shirts. A package of 5 white T-shirts costs $5.29. How much would it cost to purchase 7 packages of these T-shirts?

   _____

5. The price of a movie ticket for children under 12 is $6.75. How much would it cost for 8 ten-year-old children to go to the movies?

   _____

One-Digit by Three-Digit Multiplication

▶ Compare Multiplication Methods

Look at the drawing and the five numeric solutions for 237 × 4.

237 =	200	+	30	+	7
4	4 × 200 = 800		4 × 30 = 120		4 × 7=28

Method A	Method B	Method C	Method D	Method E
237 = 200 + 30 + 7	237 = 200 + 30 + 7	237	237	$\overset{1\,2}{237}$
× 4 =	× 4 =	× 4	× 4	× 4
4	4	———	———	———
4 × 200 = 800	800	800	28	948
4 × 30 = 120	120	120	120	
4 × 7 = 28	28	28	800	
———————	———	———	———	
948	948	948	948	

1. How are the solutions similar? List at least two ways.

_____

_____

_____

2. How are the solutions different? List at least three
   comparisons between methods.

_____

_____

_____

_____

_____

3. How do Methods A–D relate to the drawing? List at least
   two ways.

_____

_____

_____

▶ Analyze the Shortcut Method

Look at this breakdown of solution steps for Method E.

Step 1	**Step 2**	**Step 3**
$\overset{2}{237}$	$\overset{12}{237}$	$\overset{12}{237}$
$\times\ 4$	$\times\ 4$	$\times\ 4$
8	48	948

4. Describe what happens in Step 1.

_____

_____

_____

5. Describe what happens in Step 2.

_____

_____

_____

_____

6. Describe what happens in Step 3.

_____

_____

_____

Practice the Shortcut Method on these problems.

7.	349	8.	768	9.	632	10.	415
	× 6		× 9		× 7		× 3

Practice One-Digit by Three-Digit Multiplication

Class Activity

▶ Round and Estimate with Hundreds and Tens

You can use what you know about rounding and multiplication with hundreds to estimate the product of 4 × 369.

11. Find the product if you round up: 4 × 400 = _____

12. Find the product if you round down: 4 × 300 = _____

13. Which one of the two estimates will be closer to the actual solution? Why?

_____

14. Calculate the actual solution. _____

15. Explain why neither estimate is very close.

_____

_____

16. What would be the estimate if you added 50 × 4 to 300 × 4? _____

17. What would be the estimate if you added 70 × 4 to 300 × 4? _____

18. Estimate 4 × 782 by rounding 782 to the nearest hundred.

_____

19. Find the actual product. _____

20. Find a better estimate for 4 × 782. Show your work.

_____

_____

Round, estimate, and fix the estimate as needed.

21. 6 × 309

_____

_____

22. 7 × 278

_____

_____

Going Further

▶ One-Digit by Four-Digit Multiplication

You can use the multiplication methods you have learned to multiply a one-digit number by a four-digit number.

Find 8 × 3,248.

3,248 =	3,000	+	200	+	40	+	8	
8	8 × 3,000 = 24,000		8 × 200 = 1,600	8 × 40 = 320		8 × 8 = 64		8

Rectangle Sections Method

$$
\begin{aligned}
8 \times 3,000 &= 24,000 \\
8 \times 200 &= 1,600 \\
8 \times 40 &= 320 \\
8 \times 8 &= 64 \\
\hline
&25,984
\end{aligned}
$$

Expanded Notation Method

$$
\begin{aligned}
3,248 &= 3,000 + 200 + 40 + 8 \\
\times \quad 8 &= \qquad\qquad\qquad\qquad\qquad 8 \\
\hline
8 \times 3,000 &= 24,000 \\
8 \times 200 &= 1,600 \\
8 \times 40 &= 320 \\
8 \times 8 &= 64 \\
\hline
&25,984
\end{aligned}
$$

Algebraic Notation Method

$$
\begin{aligned}
8 \times 3,248 &= 8 \times (3,000 + 200 + 40 + 8) \\
&= (8 \times 3,000) + (8 \times 200) + (8 \times 40) + (8 \times 8) \\
&= 24,000 \quad + 1,600 \quad + 320 \quad + 64 \\
&= 25,984
\end{aligned}
$$

Make a rectangle drawing for each problem on your MathBoard. Then solve the problem using the method of your choice.

1. 3 × 8,153 = _____

2. 4 × 2,961 = _____

3. 6 × 5,287 = _____

4. 7 × 1,733 = _____

       Practice One-Digit by Three-Digit Multiplication

► Too Much Information

A word problem may sometimes include more information than you need. Read the following problem and then answer each question.

Mrs. Sanchez is putting a border around her garden. Her garden is a rectangle with dimensions 12 feet by 18 feet. The border material costs $3.00 per foot. How many feet of border material is needed?

1. Identify any extra numerical information. Why isn't this information needed?

   _____

   _____

2. Solve the problem. _____

Solve each problem. Cross out information that is not needed.

Show your work.

3. Judy bought a CD for $10. It has 13 songs. Each song is 3 minutes long. How long will it take to listen to the whole CD?

   _____

4. Jerry has 64 coins in his coin collection and 22 stamps in his stamp collection. His sister has 59 stamps in her collection. How many stamps do they have altogether?

   _____

5. Adrian has been playing the piano for 3 years. He practices 20 minutes a day. He is preparing for a recital that is 9 days away. How many minutes of practice will he do before the recital?

   _____

► Too Little Information

When solving problems in real life, you need to determine what information is needed to solve the problem. Read the following problem and then answer each question.

The campers and staff of a day camp are going to an amusement park on a bus. Each bus holds 26 people. How many buses will be needed?

6. Do you have enough information to solve this problem? What additional information do you need?

_____

_____

Determine if the problem can be solved. If it cannot be solved, tell what information is missing. If it can be solved, solve it.

7. Richard is saving $5 a week to buy a bike. When will he have enough money?

_____

8. Natalie wants to find out how much her cat weighs. She picks him up and steps on the scale. Together they weigh 94 pounds. How much does the cat weigh?

_____

9. Phyllis wants to make 8 potholders. She needs 36 loops for each potholder. How many loops does she need?

_____

10. For one of the problems that could not be solved, rewrite it so it can be solved and solve it.

_____

_____

▶ Discuss Problems with Hidden Questions

Mrs. Norton bought 2 packages of white cheese with 8 slices in each pack. She bought 3 packages of yellow cheese with 16 slices in each pack. How many more slices of yellow cheese than white cheese did she buy?

1. What do you need to find?

_____

_____

2. What are the hidden questions?

_____

_____

3. Answer the hidden questions to solve the problem.

How many slices of white cheese? $2 \times 8 =$ _____

How many slices of yellow cheese? $3 \times 16 =$ _____

How many more slices of yellow cheese? $48 - 16 =$ _____

Read the problem. Then answer the questions.   *Show your work.*

Maurice has 6 boxes of markers. June has 5 boxes. Each box contains 8 markers. How many markers do Maurice and June have altogether?

4. Write the hidden questions.

_____

_____

5. Solve the problem.

_____

_____

► Solve Problems with Hidden Questions

Solve each problem and show your work.
Look for hidden questions. Label your answer.

6. Mrs. Ortiz has 200 pink index cards. She has 3 packs of blue index cards with 75 cards in each pack. How many more blue index cards does she have?

_____

7. Mr. Collins counts 54 cartons and 5 boxes of paper clips. Each carton contains 8 boxes. How many boxes of paper clips does he have?

_____

8. Ms. Washington has 5 cartons of black printer ink. She has 4 cartons of color printer ink. Each carton contains 48 cartridges of ink. How many ink cartridges are there in all?

_____

9. Mrs. Arnold has 6 reams of yellow paper. She also has 5 reams of blue paper. Each ream is 500 sheets of paper. How many sheets of paper does she have altogether?

_____

10. Mr. Perez sells red, blue, pink, green, yellow, purple, silver, and gold gel pens. Each box contains 6 pens. There are 4 boxes of each color. How many gel pens does he have?

_____

▶ Compare Models

The dot drawing, area model sketch, and Rectangle Sections
Method below all model the solution to 24 × 37.

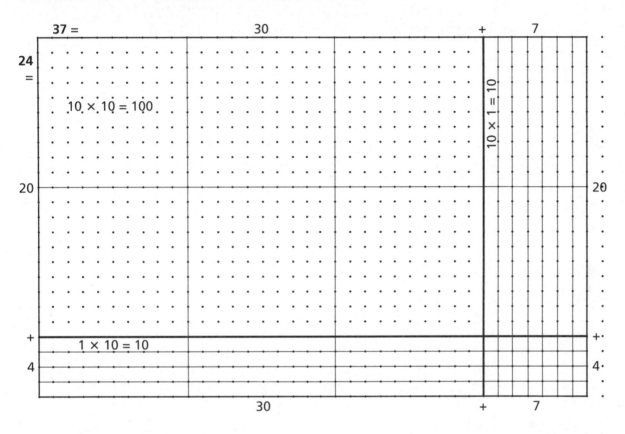

Area Model Sketch

Rectangle Sections Method

20 × 30 = **600**
20 × 7 = **140**
4 × 30 = **120**
4 × 7 = **28**

1. Describe how each model shows 6 hundreds, 14 tens,
   12 tens, and 28 ones.

_____

_____

Class Activity

▶ Investigate Products in the Sketch

Complete each equation.

2. $20 \times 30 = 2 \times 10 \times 3 \times 10$
$= 2 \times 3 \times \underline{10 \times 10}$
$= 6 \times$ _____
$=$ _____

3. $20 \times 7 = 2 \times 10 \times 7 \times 1$
$= 2 \times 7 \times \underline{10 \times 1}$
$= 14 \times$ _____
$=$ _____

4. $4 \times 30 = 4 \times 1 \times 3 \times 10$
$= 4 \times 3 \times \underline{1 \times 10}$
$= 12 \times$ _____
$=$ _____

5. $4 \times 7 = 4 \times 1 \times 7 \times 1$
$= 4 \times 7 \times \underline{1 \times 1}$
$= 28 \times$ _____
$=$ _____

6. Explain how the underlined parts in exercises 2–5 are shown in the dot drawing.

_____

_____

_____

_____

7. Find 37×24 by adding the products in exercises 2–5.

_____

▶ Practice Modeling

Use your MathBoard to sketch an area drawing for each exercise. Then find the product.

8. 36×58 _____

9. 28×42 _____

10. 63×27 _____

11. 26×57 _____

12. 86×35 _____

13. 38×65 _____

Two-Digit by Two-Digit Multiplication

► Compare Multiplication Methods

Study how these three methods of solving 43 × 67 are related to the area models.

Rectangle Sections Method

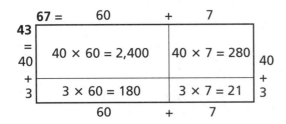

$$40 \times 60 = 2{,}400$$
$$40 \times 7 = 280$$
$$3 \times 60 = 180$$
$$\underline{3 \times 7 = 21}$$
$$2{,}881$$

Expanded Notation Method

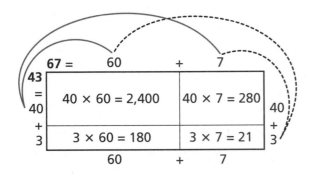

$$67 = 60 + 7$$
$$\times\ 43 = 40 + 3$$
$$\overline{}$$
$$40 \times 60 = 2{,}400$$
$$40 \times 7 = 280$$
$$3 \times 60 = 180$$
$$\underline{3 \times 7 = 21}$$
$$2{,}881$$

Algebraic Notation Method

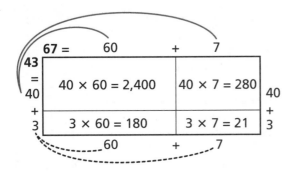

$$43 \cdot 67 = (40 + 3) \cdot (60 + 7)$$
$$= 2{,}400 + 280 + 180 + 21$$
$$= 2{,}881$$

▶ The Shortcut Method

The steps for the Shortcut Method are shown below.

Step 1	Step 2	Step 3	Step 4	Step 5
$\overset{2}{6}7$	$\overset{2}{6}7$	$\overset{\overset{2}{2}}{6}7$	$\overset{\overset{2}{2}}{6}7$	$\overset{\overset{2}{2}}{6}7$
× 43	× 43	× 43	× 43	× 43
1	201	201	201	201
		8	268	+ 268
				2,881

Explain how the area drawing below relates to the
Shortcut Method.

67

40	40 × 67 = 2,680
+ 3	3 × 67 = 201

_____

_____

_____

_____

_____

_____

_____

_____

_____

_____

Different Methods for Two-Digit Multiplication

Class Activity

▶ Estimate Products

Two-digit products can be **estimated** by **rounding** each number to the nearest ten.

Estimate and then solve.

1. 28 × 74 _____

2. 84 × 27 _____

3. 93 × 57 _____

4. 87 × 54 _____

5. 38 × 62 _____

6. 65 × 39 _____

7. 26 × 43 _____

8. 59 × 96 _____

9. 53 × 74 _____

10. Write a multiplication word problem. Estimate the product and then solve.

_____

_____

_____

_____

11. Would using an estimate be problematic in the situation you wrote for exercise 10? Explain why or why not.

_____

_____

_____

Name _____

Date _____

Going Further

▶ Multiplication and Money

You can estimate products involving money to help you plan a budget.

Estimate the amount needed and then find the exact cost.

Show your work.

1. Kate wants to give her mother a bouquet of 38 helium balloons for her thirty-eighth birthday. The cost of an inflated helium balloon is $0.75. How much would it cost to inflate 38 of them?

   _____

2. When on vacation, John wants to buy a pencil souvenir for his 32 classmates. Each pencil costs $0.38. How much would 32 pencils cost?

   _____

3. Sally's family will be taking an 18-day vacation and needs to have someone take care of their cat while they are away. A veterinarian clinic charges $12 per day to care for a cat. How much would it cost them to have this clinic care for their cat for 18 days?

   _____

4. An airline charges each passenger $87.50 for a one-way airplane ticket. If the airplane holds 72 passengers, how much can the airline earn on that flight?

   _____

5. The entrance fee to an amusement park is $13.75. How much would it cost for 27 fourth-graders to go to the park?

   _____

Check Products of Two-Digit Numbers

▶ Practice Multiplication

With practice, you will be able to solve a multiplication problem using fewer written steps.

Solve.   *Show your work.*

1. Between his ninth and tenth birthdays, Jimmy read 1 book each week. If each book had about 95 pages, about how many pages did he read during the year?

   _____

2. Sam's father built a stone wall in their back yard. The wall was 14 stones high and 79 stones long. How many stones did he use to build the wall?

   _____

3. Balloon Bonanza sells 25 different kinds of balloons. They have 48 different colors of ribbon to tie onto the balloons. How many different combinations of balloons and ribbons does Balloon Bonanza sell?

   _____

4. Brian's Bike Shop sponsors a cross-country race every summer. Every rider gets an official race T-shirt. The first year of the race, 24 riders competed. Last year, 13 times as many riders competed. If T-shirts come in boxes of 100, how many boxes of T-shirts did Brian need to have for the race last year?

   _____

Name _____ **Date** _____

Going Further

► Lattice Multiplication

Discuss how each step of the "lattice" method shown below relates to the area drawing of 43 × 67. The lattice method was used hundreds of years ago. Sometimes people traced the lattice and wrote the numbers in the ground.

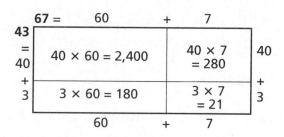

Step 1

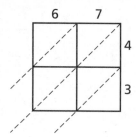

Step 2

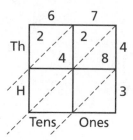

Step 3

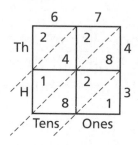

Step 4

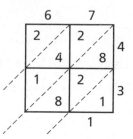

Step 5

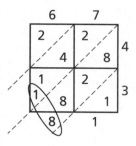

Step 6

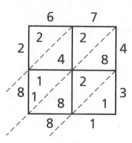

Step 7

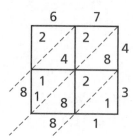

Step 8

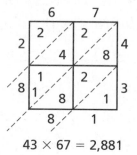

43 × 67 = 2,881

Use Lattice Multiplication to find each product.

1. 27 × 58 = _____

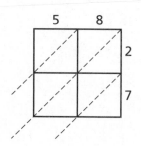

2. 65 × 87 = _____

Practice Multiplication

Class Activity

Name _____ Date _____

▶ Use Rectangles to Multiply Hundreds

You can use a model to show multiplication with hundreds.
Study this model to see how we can multiply 300 × 7.

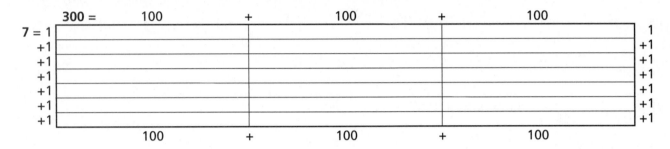

$$7 \times 300 = 7 \times (3 \times 100) = (7 \times 3) \times 100$$
$$= 21 \times 100$$
$$= 2{,}100$$

1. How many hundreds are represented in each column of the model?

   _____

2. How does knowing that 7 × 3 = 21 help you find 7 × 300?

   _____

   _____

3. What property of multiplication is used in the equation, 7 × (3 × 100) = (7 × 3) × 100?

   _____

4. Sketch a model of 400 × 6 in the space below. Be ready to explain your model.

Name _____ **Date** _____

▶ Compare Three Methods

The Rectangle Sections, Expanded Notation, and Algebraic
Method can be used to multiply numbers with hundreds.

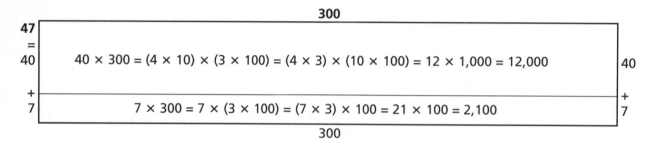

Rectangle Sections	Expanded Notation	Algebraic Method

$$\begin{array}{r} 12{,}000 \\ +\ 2{,}100 \\ \hline 14{,}100 \end{array}$$

$$\begin{array}{r} 47 = 40 + 7 \\ \times\ 300 = \quad\ \ 300 \\ \hline 300 \times 40 = 12{,}000 \\ 300 \times 7 = \ \ 2{,}100 \\ \hline 14{,}100 \end{array}$$

$$\begin{aligned} 300 \cdot 47 &= 300 \cdot (40 + 7) \\ &= (300 \cdot 40) + (300 \cdot 7) \\ &= 12{,}000 + 2{,}100 \\ &= 14{,}100 \end{aligned}$$

5. Why does each solution above finish by adding
12,000 + 2,100?

_____

_____

_____

6. How are the Expanded Notation and the Algebraic
Method alike?

_____

_____

▶ Practice Multiplication with Hundreds

Multiply using your favorite method.

7. 9 × 600 _____   **8.** 49 × 300 _____

Class Activity

▶ Use Rectangles to Multiply Thousands

You can use a model to multiply very large numbers.
Notice that each of the smaller rectangles in this model
represents one thousand. Each of the columns represents
seven one-thousands or 7,000.

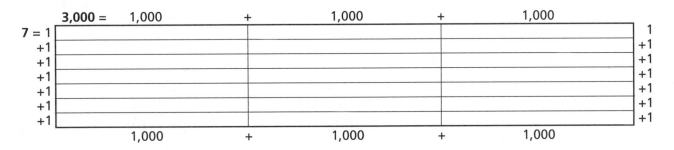

$$7 \times 3,000 = 7 \times (3 \times 1,000) = (7 \times 3) \times 1,000$$
$$= 21 \times 1,000$$
$$= 21,000$$

1. While multiplying by thousands, how many zeros can
   you expect in the product?

   _____

2. How does thinking of 3,000 as 3 × 1,000 help you to
   multiply 7 × 3,000?

   _____

   _____

   _____

   _____

3. Draw a model for 4 × 8,000. Then, find the product.

   _____

Class Activity

▶ Compare Three Methods

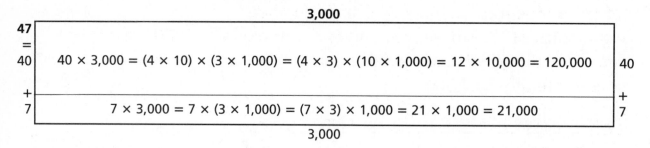

3,000
47 = 40	$40 \times 3{,}000 = (4 \times 10) \times (3 \times 1{,}000) = (4 \times 3) \times (10 \times 1{,}000) = 12 \times 10{,}000 = 120{,}000$	40
+ 7	$7 \times 3{,}000 = 7 \times (3 \times 1{,}000) = (7 \times 3) \times 1{,}000 = 21 \times 1{,}000 = 21{,}000$	+ 7

3,000

Rectangle Sections	**Expanded Notation**	**Algebraic Method**

Rectangle Sections:

$$\begin{array}{r} 120{,}000 \\ +\ 21{,}000 \\ \hline 141{,}000 \end{array}$$

Expanded Notation:

$$\begin{array}{r} 47 = 40 + 7 \\ \times\ 3{,}000 = \quad 3{,}000 \\ \hline 3{,}000 \times 40 = 120{,}000 \\ 3{,}000 \times 7 = \underline{\ 21{,}000} \\ 141{,}000 \end{array}$$

Algebraic Method:

$$3{,}000 \cdot 47 = 3{,}000 \cdot (40 + 7)$$
$$= (3{,}000 \cdot 40) + (3{,}000 \cdot 7)$$
$$= 120{,}000 + 21{,}000$$
$$= 141{,}000$$

4. How is each step in the Expanded Notation Method represented in the rectangle model?

_____

_____

_____

_____

_____

5. How are the Expanded Notation and Algebraic Method alike? How are they different?

_____

_____

_____

_____

Multiplication with Thousands

1. Use mental math to find each product.

4 × 7 _____

4 × 70 _____

40 × 70 _____

Multiply using any method. Show your work.

2. 68 × 3 _____   3. 265 × 9 _____

Estimate each product.

4. 33 × 66 _____   5. 46 × 200 _____

Solve using any method. Show your work.

6. 52 × 47 _____   7. 83 × 400 _____

Solve each problem. List any extra numerical information.

8. The fourth grade is collecting cans for a recycling center. There are 28 students in one class and 25 in another. Each student is asked to collect 15 cans. How many cans will these two classes collect in all?

   _____

9. A family spent 7 hours at the zoo. They bought 2 adult tickets for $20 each and 3 child tickets for $10 each. They bought lunch for $23. How much did the tickets cost?

   _____

10. **Extended Response** Sketch an area model for the product 23 × 6.

    Explain how the area model you drew helps you to solve the multiplication problem 23 × 6.

    _____

    _____

    _____

    _____

    _____

    _____

Class Activity

▶ **Parts of a Meter**

Find these units on your meter strip.

mm	10	20	30	40	50	60	70	80	90	100
cm	1	2	3	4	5	6	7	8	9	10
dm										1
m										

1. Find one **millimeter** (1 mm) on your strip.
   What objects are about 1 mm wide?

   _____

2. Find one **centimeter** (1 cm) on your strip.
   How many millimeters are in 1 cm?

   _____

3. What objects are about 1 cm wide?

   _____

4. Find one **decimeter** (1 dm) on your strip.
   How many centimeters are in 1 dm?

   _____

   This is one **meter** (1 m) that has been folded into
   decimeters to fit on the page.

5. How many decimeters are in 1 m?

   _____

Class Activity

Name _____ **Date** _____

▶ **Multiples of a Meter**

Vocabulary
kilometer
prefixes
metric system

Units of Length

kilometer	hectometer	decameter	meter	decimeter	centimeter	millimeter
km	hm	dam	m	dm	cm	mm
10 × 10 × 10 × larger	10 × 10 × larger	10 × larger	1 m	10 × smaller	10 × 10 × smaller	10 × 10 × 10 × smaller
1 km = 1,000 m	1 hm = 100 m	1 dam = 10 m		10 dm = 1 m	100 cm = 1 m	1,000 mm = 1 m

6. What words do you know that can help you remember what the **prefixes** mean in the **metric system**?

_____

_____

7. How do the lengths of the different units relate to each other?

_____

_____

8. How many meters are in 1 **kilometer**?

_____

9. How many millimeters are in 1 m?

_____

10. How many centimeters are in 1 m?

_____

11. What makes the metric system easy to understand?

_____

_____

▶ Choose Appropriate Units

Record which unit of length is best for measuring each object. Be prepared to justify your thinking in class.

12.

_____

13.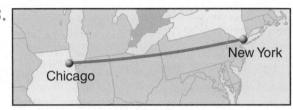

_____

14.

_____

15.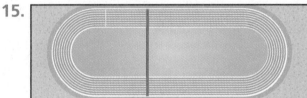

_____

16.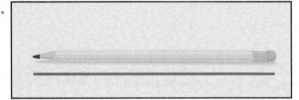

_____

17.

_____

18.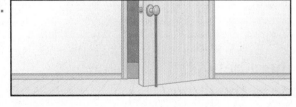

_____

19.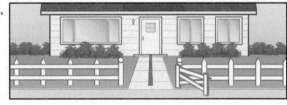

_____

Class Activity

▶ Measure Distances

The fourth-grade classes at Lincoln School are exploring metric measurements. This is a map of part of their school.

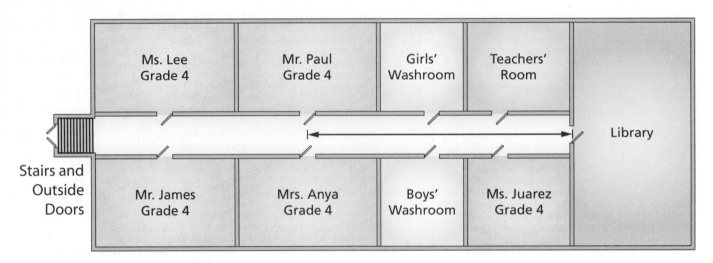

Key: ⊢—⊣ = 1 meter

Mr. Paul's students want to know the distance in whole meters between the center of their classroom door and the center of the door to the school library.

20. How can you use the map and the key to find the actual distance between two classroom doors?

_____

_____

_____

21. How many lengths of the map key are there between the door to Mr. Paul's room and the door to the library? What is that distance in meters?

_____

Dear Family,

This mini-unit is about the metric measurement system. During this unit, students will become familiar with metric units of length or distance, capacity, mass, and temperature, as well as the size of each when compared to each other.

One **meter** is about the distance an adult man can reach, or a little longer than a yard.

One **liter** is about two large glasses of liquid, or a little more than a quart.

One **gram** is about the mass of a paper clip or a single peanut. One **kilogram** is a little more than 2 pounds.

Metric temperature is measured in **Celsius** degrees (°C). Water freezes at 0°C and boils at 100°C.

Students will also discover that the metric system is based on multiples of 10. Prefixes in the names of metric measurements tell the size of a measure compared to the size of the base unit.

Units of Length						
kilometer	hectometer	decameter	meter	decimeter	centimeter	millimeter
km	hm	dam	m	dm	cm	mm
10 × 10 × 10 × larger	10 × 10 × larger	10 × larger	1 m	10 × smaller	10 × 10 × smaller	10 × 10 × 10 × smaller
1 km = 1,000 m	1 hm = 100 m	1 dam = 10 m		10 dm = 1 m	100 cm = 1 m	1,000 mm = 1 m

The most commonly used length units are the **kilometer**, **meter**, **centimeter**, and **millimeter**.

The most commonly used capacity units are the **liter** and **milliliter**.

The most commonly used units of mass are the **gram**, **kilogram**, and **milligram**.

If you have any questions or comments, please call or write to me.

Sincerely,
Your child's teacher

Carta a la familia

Estimada familia:

Esta mini unidad trata del sistema métrico de medida. Los estudiantes se familiarizarán con unidades métricas de longitud o distancia, capacidad, masa y temperatura, así como con el tamaño de cada una comparada con las otras.

Un **metro** es aproximadamente la distancia que un hombre adulto puede alcanzar extendiendo el brazo, o un poco más de una yarda.

Un **litro** es aproximadamente dos vasos grandes de líquido, o un poco más de un cuarto de galón.

Un **gramo** es aproximadamente la masa de un sujetapapeles o un cacahuate. Un **kilogramo** es un poco más de 2 libras.

La temperatura métrica se mide en grados **Celsius** (°C). El agua se congela a 0°C y hierve a 100°C.

Los estudiantes también descubrirán que el sistema métrico está basado en múltiplos de 10. Los prefijos de los nombres de las medidas métricas indican el tamaño de la medida comparado con el tamaño de la unidad base.

Unidades de longitud

kilómetro	hectómetro	decámetro	metro	decímetro	centímetro	milímetro
Km	Hm	Dm	m	dm	cm	mm
10 × 10 × 10 × más grande	10 × 10 × más grande	10 × más grande	1 m	10 × más pequeño	10 × 10 × más pequeño	10 × 10 × 10 × más pequeño
1 Km = 1,000 m	1 Hm = 100 m	1 Dm = 10 m		10 dm = 1 m	100 cm = 1 m	1,000 mm = 1 m

Las unidades de longitud más comunes son **kilómetro**, **metro**, **centímetro** y **milímetro**.

Las unidades de capacidad más comunes son **litro** y **mililitro**.

Las unidades de masa más comunes son **gramo**, **kilogramo** y **miligramo**.

Si tiene alguna pregunta o comentario, por favor comuníquese conmigo.

Atentamente,
El maestro de su niño

Measure Length and Distance

Class Activity

> **Vocabulary**
> square unit
> square meter
> square centimeter
> square millimeter
> square decimeter

► Metric Units of Area

Area is measured in **square units**, such as **square meters**.

This is one **square centimeter** (sq cm):

1. Why is it called a square unit?

_____

_____

This square centimeter is divided into **square millimeters** (sq mm):

2. How many sq mm are in 1 sq cm?

_____

This array of square centimeters is one **square decimeter** (sq dm).

3. How many square centimeters are in 1 sq dm?

_____

4. How many square millimeters are in 1 sq dm?

_____

5. How many square decimeters are in 1 sq m? Explain.

_____

_____

_____

6. How many square centimeters are in 1 sq m? How do you know?

_____

_____

Class Activity

▶ Measure Area

Ms. Juarez's students want to find the area of parts of their school.

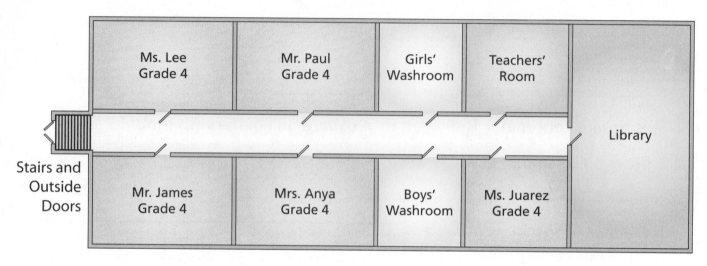

Key: ⊢─⊣ = 1 meter

7. What measurements do Ms. Juarez's students need to find the area of the hallway between the stairs and the library door?

_____

8. What do they need to do with their measurements to find the area?

_____

9. What is the area of the library?

_____

10. What is the area of the boys' and girls' washrooms combined?

_____

Class Activity

▶ **Convert Among Metric Units**

Compare units of length or distance with units of area.

Units of Area						
square kilometer	hectare	are	square meter	square decimeter	square centimeter	square millimeter
sq km	ha	a	sq m	sq dm	sq cm	sq mm
100 × 100 × 100 × larger	100 × 100 × larger	100 × larger	1 sq m	100 × smaller	100 × 100 × smaller	100 × 100 × 100 x smaller
1 sq km = 1,000,000 sq m	1 ha = 10,000 sq m	1 a = 100 sq m		100 sq dm = 1 sq m	10,000 sq cm = 1 sq m	1,000,000 sq mm = 1 sq m

Solve.

11. How many meters long is each side of a square
    that has an area of 4 square meters (sq m)?

    _____

12. How many one-meter squares cover a square
    that has an area of 4 square meters (sq m)?

    _____

13. How many meters long is each side of a square
    that has an area of 4 **square kilometers** (sq km)?

    _____

14. How many one-meter squares cover a square
    that has an area of 4 sq km?

    _____

15. How is a square measurement unit like a square number
    in multiplication?

    _____

    _____

Going Further

▶ Use a Simpler Problem

To solve a more difficult problem, sometimes you can think about a simpler problem.

1. Manuel cuts a length of rug into pieces of equal area.
   He cuts 8 square pieces like the one shown.

   16 m

   2 m

   What is the area of each piece of rug? _____

   Hint: What would the answer be if he made just one cut? two cuts?

2. Adita used square tiles to make a design.
   The sides of her tiles are 5 centimeters. She
   made a square design using 36 of the tiles.
   What was the perimeter of her design? _____

   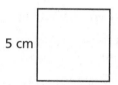

   5 cm

   Hint: What would the perimeter be if she used one-centimeter square tiles?

3. Adita used red and yellow tiles for her design in
   problem 2. She used one yellow tile for every
   three red tiles. How many of each color did she use?

   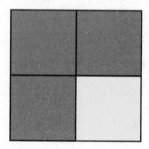

   _____

4. How many different ways can you name a line segment
   using any 2 of the first 8 letters of the alphabet?

   _____

   A   B

Name _____   Date _____

▶ Visualize a Cubic Meter

The basic metric unit for measuring **volume** is a **cubic meter**.

This is a **cubic centimeter**.

Units of Volume			
cubic meter	cubic decimeter	cubic centimeter	cubic millimeter
cu m	cu dm	cu cm	cu mm
1 cu m	1,000 × smaller	1,000 × 1,000 × smaller	1,000 × 1,000 × 1,000 × smaller
	1,000 cu dm = 1 cu m	1,000,000 cu cm = 1 cu m	1,000,000,000 cu mm = 1 cu m

1. How many centimeters are equal to one meter? _____

2. How many cubic centimeters do you think you will need for a cubic meter?

_____

3. What pattern do you see in the metric units of volume in the chart?

_____

▶ Measure Volume

Each student at Lincoln School has a coat locker. Each locker is 1 meter high, 3 decimeters deep, and 5 decimeters across.

4. How can you find the total space inside a student locker?

_____

_____

_____

5. What is the volume of each locker? _____

Class Activity

Name _____ **Date** _____

Vocabulary
capacity
liter
milliliter
kiloliter

▶ Measure Capacity

The base metric unit of **capacity** is a **liter**.

Units of Capacity						
kiloliter	hectoliter	decaliter	liter	deciliter	centiliter	milliliter
kL	hL	daL	L	dL	cL	mL
10 × 10 × 10 × larger	10 × 10 × larger	10 × larger	1 L	10 × smaller	10 × 10 × smaller	10 × 10 × 10 x smaller
1 kL = 1,000 L	1 hL = 100 L	1 daL = 10 L		10 dL = 1 L	100 cL = 1 L	1,000 mL = 1 L

Ms. Lee's class cut a two-liter plastic bottle in half to make a one-liter jar. They marked the outside to show equal parts.

6. How many **milliliters** of water will fit in the jar?

_____

7. How many of these jars will fill a **kiloliter** container? Explain why.

_____

_____

Here is a picture of a cubic centimeter.

If you could fill one cubic centimeter with water, you would have 1 milliliter (mL) of water.

8. How many cubic centimeters of water will Ms. Lee's jar hold? Explain why.

_____

_____

9. How many liters of water will fill a cubic decimeter?

_____

Measure Volume and Capacity

Class Activity

Vocabulary	
mass	tonne
gram	milligram
kilogram	

▶ **Measure Mass**

The basic unit of **mass** is the **gram**.

Units of Mass						
kilogram	hectogram	decagram	gram	decigram	centigram	milligram
kg	hg	dag	g	dg	cg	mg
10 × 10 × 10 × larger	10 × 10 × larger	10 × larger	1 g	10 × smaller	10 × 10 × smaller	10 × 10 × 10 × smaller
1 kg = 1,000 g	1 hg = 100 g	1 dag = 10 g		10 dg = 1 g	100 cg = 1 g	1,000 mg = 1 g

1. How many **milligrams** are equal to 1 gram?

_____

2. How many grams are equal to 1 kilogram?

_____

Here is a picture of a cubic centimeter. You know that
1 cu cm can hold 1 mL of water. If you could weigh
that amount of water, its mass would be one gram (1 g).

3. Is the gram a small or large unit of measurement?
Explain your thinking.

_____

Another common metric unit of mass is a **tonne**. It is equal
to 1,000 **kilograms**.

4. How many grams are in a tonne?

_____

5. Why is this very large unit of mass useful?

_____

_____

6. What might you measure in tonnes?

_____

► Interpret a Bar Graph

Mrs. Anya's students graphed the weights of different dogs in the animal shelter.

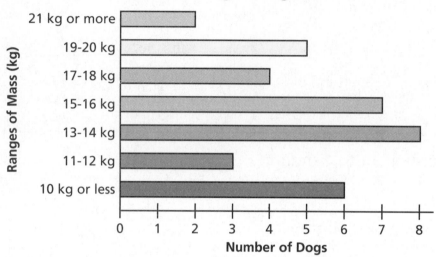

Mass of Dogs Weighed

7. How many dogs weighed 10 kilograms or less? _____

8. How many dogs weighed 21 kilograms or more? _____

9. Compare the number of dogs that weighed the most to the number of dogs that weighed the least. Describe the comparison as many ways as you can.

_____

_____

_____

10. Write two different comparison statements about the dogs.

_____

_____

_____

Name _____ **Date** _____

▶ **Explore the Celsius Scale**

The common temperature scale in the U.S. is called
Fahrenheit (°F). The metric temperature scale is called
Celsius (°C).

Equivalent Temperatures in Celsius and Fahrenheit

Temperature (°C)	−20	−10	0	10	20	30	40	50	60	70	80	90	100	110	120	130
Temperature (°F)	−4	14	32	50	68	86	104	122	140	158	176	194	212	230	248	266

1. What is the range of the Celsius temperatures on the table?

_____

2. What is the range of the Fahrenheit temperatures on the table?

_____

3. What happens to water at 32°F? What Celsius temperature is equivalent to 32°F?

_____

4. What happens to water at 212°F? What Celsius temperature is equivalent to 212°F?

_____

5. The temperature sign outside a bank reads 50°. Is this temperature a Celsius or a Fahrenheit reading? Explain.

_____

_____

6. If a Celsius thermometer shows 8°, what kind of clothing should you wear to be comfortable?

_____

7. If puddles of water have a thin coating of ice on them, what is a reasonable estimate of the Celsius temperature?

_____

8. A digital body thermometer says your body temperature is 39°C. Do you have a fever? How do you know?

_____

○▶ Write Equivalent Temperatures

Write an equivalent temperature. Use the chart on the previous page.

9. 40°F _____

10. 75°F _____

11. 0°F _____

12. 15°C _____

13. 35°C _____

14. −15°C _____

▶ Relate Celsius Temperatures to Everyday Experiences

Each day of the school year, Mr. James's students measure the outside temperature in degrees Celsius (°C). They made a table of their results. This table shows four sample weeks from different times of the year.

Days	Week A					Week B					Week C					Week D				
	M	T	W	Th	F	M	T	W	Th	F	M	T	W	Th	F	M	T	W	Th	F
Temp. (°C)	−20	−19	−18	−4	−8	6	5	8	4	9	13	15	18	21	18	28	31	27	25	29

15. How is the temperature during Week A different from the temperature in Week D?

_____

_____

_____

16. In your city, what month or months of the year could each week represent? Explain your thinking.

_____

_____

_____

Measure Temperature

Write the best metric unit for each situation. Explain your thinking.

1. the length across a dime

_____

_____

_____

2.  the amount of water a pool can hold

_____

_____

_____

3.  the distance between two cities

_____

_____

_____

4.  the temperature of an oven

_____

_____

_____

Name _____ **Date** _____

Write the correct metric unit to complete the equation.

5. 1 meter = 100 _____

6. 1,000 millimeters = 1 _____

7. 10 liters = 10,000 _____

8. 1,000 grams = 1 _____

Cassie entered the triple jump event at her school's field day. She made 3 attempts. Use this information to solve these word problems.

9. In her first attempt, Cassie jumped 1,210 cm in total. In her second attempt, she jumped 1,180 cm in total. How much farther, in centimeters, did she jump on the better of the two attempts?

   _____

10. **Extended Response** In her third attempt, Cassie jumped 48 dm, 340 cm, and 4 m. What is the total distance, in centimeters, that Cassie jumped? Explain your answer.

   _____

   _____

   _____

Show your work.

Glossary

A

acre A measure of land area. An acre is equal to 4,840 square yards.

acute angle An angle smaller than a right angle.

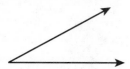

acute triangle A triangle with three acute angles.

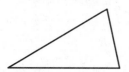

addend One of two or more numbers added together to find a sum.

Example:

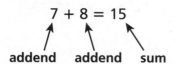

analog clock A clock with a face and hands.

angle A figure formed by two rays with the same endpoint.

array An arrangement of objects, symbols, or numbers in rows and columns.

area The amount of surface covered or enclosed by a figure measured in square units.

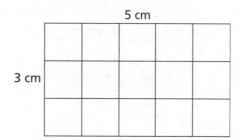

Associative Property of Addition Grouping the addends in different ways does not change the sum.

Example: $3 + (5 + 7) = 15$
$(3 + 5) + 7 = 15$

Associative Property of Multiplication Grouping the factors in different ways does not change the product.

Example: $3 \times (5 \times 7) = 105$
$(3 \times 5) \times 7 = 105$

Glossary (Continued)

average (mean) The size of each of *n* equal groups made from *n* data values. It is calculated by adding the values and dividing by *n*.

Example: 75, 84, 89, 91, 101
75 + 84 + 89 + 91 + 101 = 440,
then 440 ÷ 5 = 88. The average is 88.

B

bar graph A graph that uses bars to show data. The bars may be vertical or horizontal.

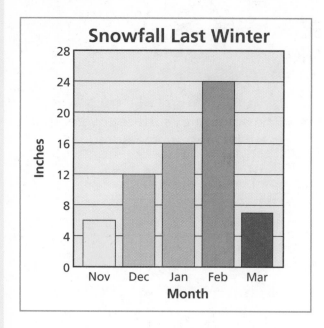

base For a triangle or parallelogram, a base is any side. For a trapezoid, a base is either of the parallel sides. For a prism, a base is one of the congruent parallel faces that may not be rectangular. For a pyramid, the base is the face that does not touch the vertex of the pyramid.

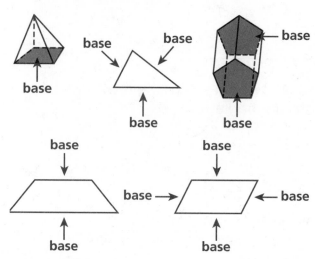

break-apart drawing A diagram that shows two addends and the sum.

81
72 9

C

capacity A measure of how much a container can hold.

Celsius The metric temperature scale.

center The point that is the same distance from every point on the circle.

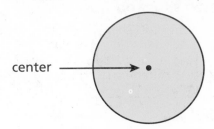

center

centimeter A unit of measure in the metric system that equals one hundredth of a meter. 1 cm = 0.01 m

change minus A change situation that can be represented by subtraction. In a change minus situation, the starting number, the change, or the result will be unknown.

Example:

Unknown Start	Unknown Change	Unknown Result
$n - 2 = 3$	$5 - n = 3$	$5 - 2 = n$

change plus A change situation that can be represented by addition. In a change plus situation, the starting number, the change, or the result will be unknown.

Example:

Unknown Start	Unknown Change	Unknown Result
$n + 2 = 5$	$3 + n = 5$	$3 + 2 = n$

circle A plane figure that forms a closed path so that all the points on the path are the same distance from a point called the center.

circle graph A graph that uses parts of a circle to show data.

Example:

Favorite Fiction Books

circumference The distance around a circle.

closed Having no endpoints.

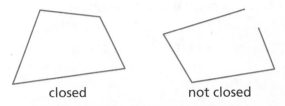

closed   not closed

Collection Situations Situations that involve putting together (joining) or taking apart (separating) groups.

column A part of a table or array that contains items arranged vertically.

● ● ● ●
● ● ● ●
● ● ● ●
● ● ● ●

Glossary (Continued)

combination situation A situation in which the number of possible different combinations is determined. A table can sometimes be used to show all possible combinations; multiplication can be used to calculate the number of combinations.

Example:

Different Sandwich Combinations

	peanut butter	cheese	turkey
wheat bread	peanut butter on wheat bread	cheese on wheat bread	turkey on wheat bread
white bread	peanut butter on white bread	cheese on white bread	turkey on white bread

Number of combinations = 3 × 2 = 6

common denominator A common multiple of two or more denominators.

Example: A common denominator of $\frac{1}{2}$ and $\frac{1}{3}$ is 6 because 6 is a multiple of 2 and 3.

Commutative Property of Addition Changing the order of addends does not change the sum.

Example: 3 + 8 = 11
8 + 3 = 11

Commutative Property of Multiplication Changing the order of factors does not change the product.

Example: 3 × 8 = 24
8 × 3 = 24

comparison bars Bars that represent the larger amount and smaller amount in a comparison situation.

For addition and subtraction:

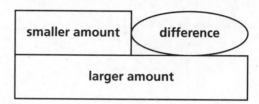

For multiplication and division:

smaller amount	smaller amount	smaller amount	larger amount

smaller amount			

comparison situation A situation in which two amounts are compared by addition or by multiplication. An additive comparison situation compares by asking or telling how much more (how much less) one amount is than another. A multiplicative comparison situation compares by asking or telling how many times as many one amount is as another. The multiplicative comparison may also be made using fraction language. For example, you can say, "Sally has one fourth as much as Tom has," instead of saying "Tom has 4 times as much as Sally has."

complex figure A figure made by combining simple geometric figures like rectangles and triangles. The factor pairs of 18 are 1 and 18, 2 and 9, 3 and 6.

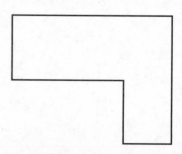

composite number A number greater than 1 that has more than one factor pair. Examples of composite numbers are 10 and 18. The factor pairs of 10 are 1 and 10, 2 and 5. The factor pairs of 18 are 1 and 18, 2 and 9, 3 and 6.

concave A polygon is concave if the inside angle for at least one vertex is greater than 180°.

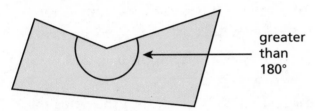

greater than 180°

cone A solid figure with a curved base and a single vertex.

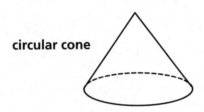

circular cone

congruent Exactly the same size and shape.

Example: Triangles *ABC* and *PQR* are congruent.

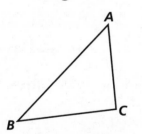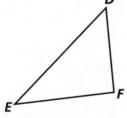

A   D

B   C   E   F

convex A polygon is convex if each inside angle measures less than 180°.

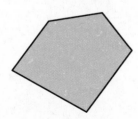

cube A solid figure that has 6 faces that are congruent squares.

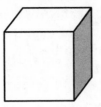

cubic centimeter A metric unit for measuring volume. It is the volume of a cube with one-centimeter edges.

cubic foot A unit for measuring volume. It is the volume of a cube with one-foot edges.

cubic inch A unit for measuring volume. It is the volume of a cube with one-inch edges.

cubic meter A metric unit for measuring volume. It is the volume of a cube with one-meter edges.

cubic yard A unit for measuring volume. It is the volume of a cube with one-yard edges.

cylinder A solid figure with two congruent curved bases.

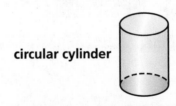

circular cylinder

D

data A collection of information.

Glossary (Continued)

decimal number A representation of a number using the numerals 0 to 9, in which each digit has a value 10 times the digit to its right. A dot or **decimal point** separates the whole-number part of the number on the left from the fractional part on the right.

Examples: 1.23 and 0.3

decimal point A symbol used to separate dollars and cents in money amounts or to separate ones and tenths in decimal numbers.

Examples:

decimal point

decimeter A unit of measure in the metric system that equals one tenth of a meter. 1 dm = 0.1 m

denominator The number below the bar in a fraction. It shows the total number of equal parts in the fraction.

Example:

$\frac{3}{4}$ ◄—— denominator

diagonal A line segment that connects vertices of a polygon, but is not a side of the polygon.

diagonal

diameter A line segment from one side of a circle to the other through the center. Also the length of that segment.

difference The result of a subtraction.

Example: 54 − 37 = 17 ← difference

digit Any of the symbols 0, 1, 2, 3, 4, 5, 6, 7, 8, or 9.

digital clock A clock that shows us the hour and minutes with numbers

Digit-by-Digit A method used to solve a division problem.

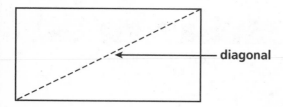

Put in only one digit at a time.

$$
\begin{array}{r}
5 \\
7{\overline{\smash{\big)}\,3{,}822}} \\
-35 \\
\hline
32
\end{array}
\qquad
\begin{array}{r}
54 \\
7{\overline{\smash{\big)}\,3{,}822}} \\
-35 \\
\hline
32 \\
-28 \\
\hline
42
\end{array}
\qquad
\begin{array}{r}
546 \\
7{\overline{\smash{\big)}\,3{,}822}} \\
-35 \\
\hline
32 \\
-28 \\
\hline
42 \\
-42
\end{array}
$$

dimension The height, length, or width.

Examples:
A line segment has only length, so it has *one* dimension.
A rectangle has length and width, so it has *two* dimensions.
A cube has length, width, and height, so it has *three* dimensions.

Distributive Property You can multiply a sum by a number, or multiply each addend by the number and add the products; the result is the same.

Example:
$$3 \times (2 + 4) = (3 \times 2) + (3 \times 4)$$
$$3 \times 6 = 6 + 12$$
$$18 = 18$$

dividend The number that is divided in division.

Example: $9\overline{)63}$, 63 is the dividend.

divisor The number you divide by in division.

Example: $9\overline{)63}$, 9 is the divisor.

dot array An arrangement of dots in rows and columns.

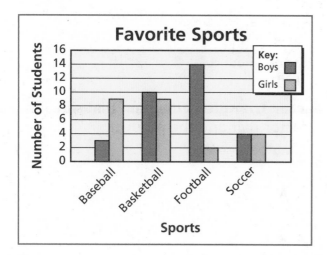

double bar graph Data is compared by using pairs of bars drawn next to each other.

Favorite Sports

Number of Students vs Sports (Baseball, Basketball, Football, Soccer)
Key: Boys, Girls

---

edge The line segment where two faces of a three-dimensional figure meet.

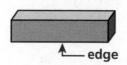
edge

equally likely In probability, equally likely means having the same chance of occurring.

Example: When flipping a coin, the coin is **equally likely** to land on heads or tails.

Equal-Shares Drawing A diagram that shows a number separated into equal parts.

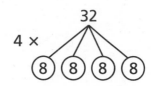

$4 \times$ 32 → 8   8   8   8

equation A statement that two expressions are equal. It has an equals sign.

Examples: $32 + 35 = 67$
$67 = 32 + 34 + 1$
$(7 \times 8) + 1 = 57$

equilateral Having all equal sides.

Example: An equilateral triangle

equivalent fractions Two or more fractions that represent the same number.

Example: $\frac{2}{4}$ and $\frac{4}{8}$ are equivalent because they both represent one half.

Glossary (Continued)

estimate A number close to an exact amount or to find about how many or how much.

expanded form A way of writing a number that shows the value of each of its digits.

Example: Expanded form of 835:
800 + 30 + 5
8 hundreds + 3 tens + 5 ones

Expanded Notation A method used to solve multiplication and division problems.

Examples:

| 43 × 67 |

```
        67 = 60 + 7
      × 43 = 40 + 3
  40 × 60 = 2400
  40 × 7  =  280
   3 × 60 =  180
   3 × 7  = + 21
              2,881
```

| 3,822 ÷ 7 |

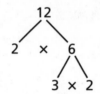

```
       6
      40 )546
     500
   7 ) 3,822
     − 3 500
         322
       − 280
          42
        − 42
           0
```

expression One or more numbers, variables, or numbers and variables with one or more operations.

Examples: 4
6x
6x − 5
7 + 4

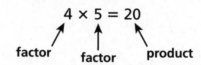

face A flat surface of a three-dimensional figure.

factor One of two or more numbers multiplied to find a product.

Example:

$$4 \times 5 = 20$$

factor   factor   product

Factor Fireworks Shows how a whole number can be broken down into a product of prime factors.

12

2 × 6

3 × 2

This is also called a **Factor Tree.**

factor pair A factor pair for a number is a pair of whole numbers whose product is that number.

Example:

$$5 \times 7 = 35$$

factor   product
pair

Factor Triangle A diagram that shows a factor pair and the product.

Example:

32

÷ /\ ÷

4 × 8

Fahrenheit The temperature scale used in the United States.

Fast Array A numerical form of an array that shows an unknown factor or unknown product.

```
        4
      o o o o
        o
   6    o
        o   24
        o
        o
        o
```

```
         8
   o━━━━━━━━━━━━
   3  o   24
      o
```

foot A U.S. customary unit of length equal to 12 inches.

fraction A number that is the sum of unit fractions, each an equal part of a set or part of a whole.

Examples: $\frac{3}{4} = \frac{1}{4} + \frac{1}{4} + \frac{1}{4}$

$\frac{5}{4} = \frac{1}{4} + \frac{1}{4} + \frac{1}{4} + \frac{1}{4} + \frac{1}{4}$

frequency table A table that shows how many times each event, item, or category occurs.

Frequency Table	
Height	Frequency
47	1
48	2
49	4
50	3
51	1
52	0
53	2
Total	13

function A set of ordered pairs of numbers such that for every first number there is only one possible second number.

Example: The relationship between yards and feet.

Yards	1	2	3	4	5	6	7
Feet	3	6	9	12	15	18	21

function table A table of ordered pairs that shows a function.

Rule: add 2	
Input	Output
1	3
2	4
3	5
4	6

Heads	1	2	3	4
Legs	2	4	6	8

G

gram The basic unit of mass in the metric system.

greater than (>) A symbol used to compare two numbers. The greater number is given first below.

Example: 33 > 17
33 is greater than 17.

greatest Largest. Used to order three or more quantities or numbers.

H

height The perpendicular distance from a base of a figure to the highest point.

horizontal bar graph A bar graph with horizontal bars.

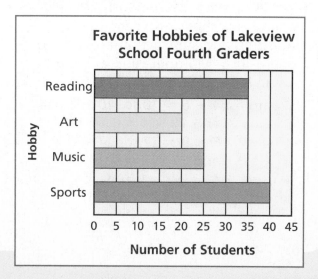

Glossary (Continued)

hundredth A unit fraction representing one of one hundred parts, written as 0.01 or $\frac{1}{100}$.

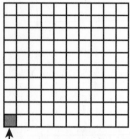

hundredth

one hundredth = $\frac{1}{100}$ = 0.01

I

Identity Property of Multiplication The product of 1 and any number equals that number.

Example: $10 \times 1 = 10$

improper fraction A fraction that is greater than or equal to 1. The numerator is greater than or equal to the denominator.

Examples: $\frac{13}{4}$ or $\frac{4}{4}$

inch A U.S. customary unit of length.

Example: 1 inch

inequality A statement that two expressions are not equal.

Examples: $2 < 5$
$4 + 5 > 12 - 8$

inverse operations Opposite or reverse operations that undo each other. Addition and subtraction are inverse operations. Multiplication and division are inverse operations.

Examples: $4 + 6 = 10$ so, $10 - 6 = 4$
and $10 - 4 = 6$.
$3 \times 9 = 27$ so, $27 \div 9 = 3$
and $27 \div 3 = 9$.

isosceles trapezoid A trapezoid with a pair of opposite congruent sides.

isosceles triangle A triangle with at least two congruent sides.

K

kilogram A unit of mass in the metric system that equals one thousand grams. 1 kg = 1,000 g

kiloliter A unit of capacity in the metric system that equals one thousand liters. 1 kL = 1,000 L

L

least Smallest. Used to order three or more quantities or numbers.

least common denominator The least common multiple of two or more denominators.

Example: The least common denominator of $\frac{1}{2}$ and $\frac{1}{6}$ is 6 because 6 is the smallest multiple of 2 and 3.

length The measure of a line segment.

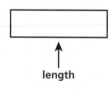

length

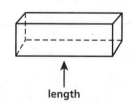

length

less than (<) A symbol used to compare two numbers. The smaller number is given first below.

Example: 54 < 78
54 is less than 78.

line A straight path that goes on forever in opposite directions.

Example: line *AB*

line of symmetry A line that divides a figure into two congruent parts.

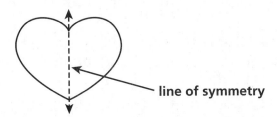

line of symmetry

line plot A diagram that shows the frequency of data on a number line.

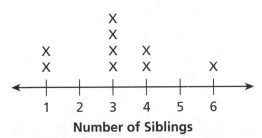

line segment Part of a line that has two endpoints.

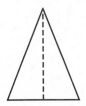

line symmetry A figure has line symmetry if it can be folded along a line to create two halves that match exactly.

liter The basic unit of capacity in the metric system. 1 liter = 1,000 milliliters.

M

mass The measure of the amount of matter in an object.

mean (average) The size of each of *n* equal groups made from *n* data values. It is calculated by adding the values and dividing by *n*.

Examples: 75, 84, 89, 91, 101
75 + 84 + 89 + 91 + 101 = 440,
then 440 ÷ 5 = 88. The mean is 88.

measure of central tendency The mean, median, or mode of a set of numbers.

median The middle number in a set of ordered numbers. For an even number of numbers, the median is the average of the two middle numbers.

Examples: 13 26 34 47 52
The median for this set is 34.

8 8 12 14 20 21
The median for this set is
(12 + 14) ÷ 2 = 13.

meter The basic unit of length in the metric system.

mile A U.S. customary unit of length equal to 5,280 feet.

milligram A unit of mass in the metric system that equals one thousandth of a gram. 1 mg = 0.001 g

milliliter A unit of capacity in the metric system that equals one thousandth of a liter. 1 mL = 0.001 L

millimeter A unit of length in the metric system that equals one thousandth of a meter. 1 mm = 0.001 m

Glossary (Continued)

misleading A comparing sentence containing language that may trick you into doing the wrong operation.

Example: John's age is 3 *more than* Jessica's. If John is 12, how old is Jessica?

mixed number A number that can be represented by a whole number and a fraction.

Example: $4\frac{1}{2}$

mode The number that appears most frequently in a set of numbers.

Example: 2, 4, 4, 4, 5, 7, 7
4 is the mode in this set of numbers.

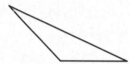

net A flat pattern that can be folded to make a solid figure.

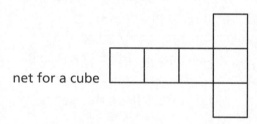

net for a cube

number sentence A mathematical statement that uses =, <, or > to show how numbers or expressions are related. The types of number sentences are equations and inequalities.

Example: 25 + 25 = 50
13 > 8 + 2

numerator The number above the bar in a fraction. It shows the number of equal parts.

Example:

$\frac{3}{4}$ ← numerator $\frac{3}{4} = \frac{1}{4} + \frac{1}{4} + \frac{1}{4}$

obtuse angle An angle greater than a right angle and less than a straight angle.

obtuse triangle A triangle with one obtuse angle.

Order of Operations A set of rules that state the order in which operations should be done.

STEPS: -Compute inside parentheses first.
    -Multiply and divide from left to right.
    -Add and subtract from left to right.

ounce A unit of weight equal to one sixteenth of a pound. A unit of capacity equal to one eighth of a cup (also called a fluid ounce).

P

parallel Lines in the same plane that never intersect are parallel. Line segments and rays that are part of parallel lines are also parallel.

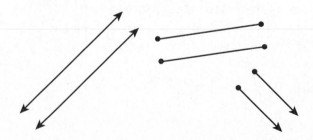

parallelogram A quadrilateral with both pairs of opposite sides parallel.

Partial-Quotients Method A method used to solve division problems where the partial quotients are written next to the division problem instead of above it.

Example:

$$
\begin{array}{r|r}
8\overline{)178} & \\
-\ 160 & 20 \\
\hline
18 & \\
-\ 16 & 2 \\
\hline
2 & 22 \\
\end{array}
$$

22 R2

pentagon A polygon with five sides.

perimeter The distance around a figure.

perpendicular Lines, line segments, or rays are perpendicular if they form right angles.

Example: These two line segments are perpendicular.

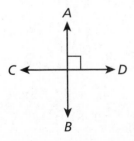

pi A special number equal to the circumference of a circle divided by its diameter. Pi can be represented by the symbol π and is approximately 3.14.

pictograph A graph that uses pictures or symbols to represent data.

Minutes Studied	
Student	
Najee	📖 📖
Tariq	📖 📖 📖 📖 📖 📖
Celine	📖 📖 📖 📖 📖 📖 📖 📖
Jamarcus	📖 📖 📖
Brooke	📖 📖 📖 📖

📖 = 5 minutes

place value The value assigned to the place that a digit occupies in a number.

Example: 2̲35

The 2 is in the hundreds place, so its value is 200.

plane A flat surface that extends without end.

polygon A closed plane figure with sides made of straight line segments.

pound A unit of weight in the U.S. customary system.

prime number A number greater than 1 that has 1 and itself as the only factor pair. Examples of prime numbers are 2, 7, and 13. The only factor pair of 7 is 1 and 7.

prism A solid figure with two congruent parallel bases joined by rectangular faces. Prisms are named by the shape of their bases.

pentagonal prism

probability A number between 0 and 1 that represents the chance of an event happening.

Glossary (Continued)

product The answer to a multiplication.

Example: $9 \times 7 = 63$

product

pyramid A solid with a polygon for a base whose faces meet at a point called the vertex.

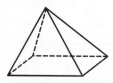

Q

quadrilateral A polygon with four sides.

quotient The answer to a division problem.

Example: $9\overline{)63}$; 7 is the quotient.

R

radius A line segment that connects the center of a circle to any point on that circle. Also the length of that line segment.

range The difference between the greatest number and the least number in a set.

ray Part of a line that has one endpoint and extends without end in one direction.

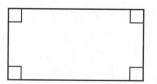

rectangle A parallelogram with four right angles.

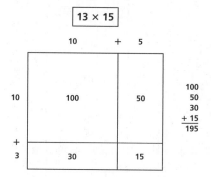

Rectangle Sections A method using rectangle drawings to solve multiplication or division problems.

| 13 × 15 |

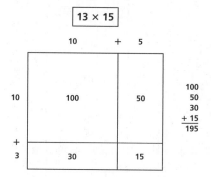

reflection A transformation that flips a figure onto a congruent image. Sometimes called a *flip*.

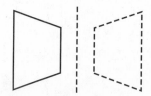

regular polygon Having all sides and angles congruent.

Example: A square is a regular quadrilateral.

remainder The number left over after dividing two numbers that are not evenly divisible.

Example: $5\overline{)43}$ 8 R3   The remainder is 3.

Repeated Groups situation A multiplication situation in which all groups have the same number of objects.

rhombus A parallelogram with congruent sides.

right angle One of four congruent angles made by perpendicular lines.

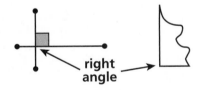

right angle

right triangle A triangle with one right angle.

round To find the nearest ten, hundred, thousand, or some other place value. The usual rounding rule is to round up if the next digit to the right is 5 or more and round down if the next digit to the right is less than 5.

Examples: 463 rounded to the nearest ten is 460.
463 rounded to the nearest hundred is 500.

row A part of a table or array that contains items arranged horizontally.

S

scalene A triangle with no equal sides is a scalene triangle.

simplest form A fraction is in simplest form if there is no whole number (other than 1) that divides evenly into the numerator and denominator.

Examples: $\frac{3}{4}$ This fraction is in simplest form because no number divides evenly into 3 and 4.

Glossary (Continued)

simplify a fraction To divide the numerator and the denominator of a fraction by the same number to make an equivalent fraction made from fewer but larger unit fractions.

Example: $\frac{5}{10} = \frac{5 \div 5}{10 \div 5} = \frac{1}{2}$

situation equation An equation that shows the action or the relationship in a problem.

Example: $35 + n = 40$

slant height The height of a triangular face of a pyramid.

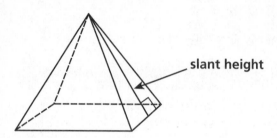

slant height

solution equation An equation that shows the operation to perform in order to solve the problem.

Examples: $n = 40 - 35$

sphere A solid figure shaped like a ball.

square array An array in which the number of rows equals the number of columns.

● ● ● ● ●
● ● ● ● ●
● ● ● ● ●
● ● ● ● ●
● ● ● ● ●

square centimeter A unit of area equal to the area of a square with one-centimeter sides.

square decimeter A unit of area equal to the area of a square with one-decimeter sides.

square foot A unit of area equal to the area of a square with one-foot sides.

square inch A unit of area equal to the area of a square with one-inch sides.

square kilometer A unit of area equal to the area of a square with one-kilometer sides.

square meter A unit of area equal to the area of a square with one-meter sides.

square mile A unit of area equal to the area of a square with one-mile sides.

square millimeter A unit of area equal to the area of a square with one-millimeter sides.

square number The product of a whole number and itself.

Example: $3 \times 3 = 9$
9 is a square number.

square unit A unit of area equal to the area of a square with one-unit sides.

square yard A unit of area equal to the area of a square with one-yard sides.

standard form The form of a number written using digits.

Example: 2,145

sum The answer when adding two or more addends.

Example:

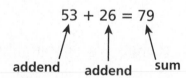

$$53 + 26 = 79$$

addend   addend   sum

surface area The total area of the two-dimensional surfaces of a three-dimensional figure.

table Data arranged in rows and columns.

tally chart A chart that uses tally marks to record and organize data.

Tally Chart	
Height (inches)	Tally
47	///
48	ﬀﬀ
49	//
50	
51	ﬀﬀ /
52	////
53	//

/ is 1

ﬀﬀ is 5

tenth A unit fraction representing one of ten equal parts of a whole, written as 0.1 or $\frac{1}{10}$.

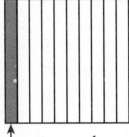

one tenth = $\frac{1}{10}$ = 0.1

12.34
↑
tenth

thousandth A unit fraction representing one of one thousand equal parts of a whole, written as 0.001 or $\frac{1}{1,000}$.

ton A unit of weight that equals 2,000 pounds.

total Sum. The result of addition.

Example:

$$53 + 26 = 79$$

addend   addend   total (sum)

translation A transformation that moves a figure along a straight line without turning or flipping. Sometimes called a *slide*.

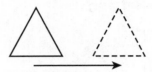

trapezoid A quadrilateral with one pair of parallel sides.

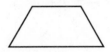

triangle A polygon with three sides.

unit A standard of measurement.

Examples: Centimeters, pounds, inches, and so on.

unit fraction A fraction whose numerator is 1. It shows one equal part of a whole.

Example: $\frac{1}{4}$

vertex A point that is shared by two sides of an angle, two sides of a polygon, or edges of a solid figure.

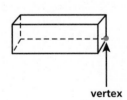

vertex   vertex   vertex

Glossary (Continued)

vertical bar graph A bar graph with vertical bars.

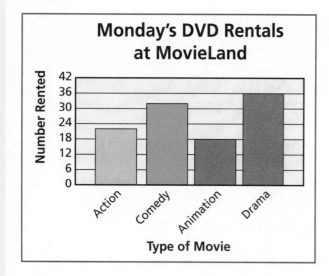

volume The number of cubic units of space occupied by a solid figure.

width The measure of one side or edge of a figure.

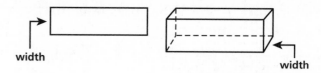

word form The form of a number written using words instead of digits.

Example: Six hundred thirty-nine

yard A U.S. customary unit of length equal to 3 feet.